# building a
# YOUNG ADULT
# MINISTRY

# building a
# YOUNG ADULT
# MINISTRY

## Larry A. LeFeber

Judson Press ® Valley Forge

**BUILDING A YOUNG ADULT MINISTRY**

Copyright © 1980
Judson Press, Valley Forge, PA 19481

Unless otherwise indicated, Bible quotations in this volume are from the Revised Standard Version of the Bible, copyrighted 1946, 1952, 1971, 1973 © by the Division of Christian Education of the National Council of the Churches of Christ in the United States of America, and are used by permission.

**Library of Congress Cataloging in Publication Data**
LeFeber, Larry A.
    Building a young adult ministry.

    Bibliography: p. 121
    Includes index.
    1. Church work with young adults. I. Title.
BV4446.L43        259        79-19215
ISBN 0-8170-0848-9

The name JUDSON PRESS is registered as a trademark in the U.S. Patent Office.
Printed in the U.S.A.  ⊕

## DEDICATION

This book is dedicated to all persons who are seriously considering an initial or a deepened involvement in the field of young adult ministry, and also to the promising possibilities for the Christian church which can come as a result of these ventures.

# Acknowledgments

I want to say "thank you" to my wife, Bette Rae, for the long hours of typing and proofreading, and for her trusted advice; to our children, Amy and Eric, for understanding that this work entailed much of Mom and Dad's time; to all of the persons in four ministry settings who have provided the rich experiences out of which this book could be written; and finally, to God, for the strength and the inspiration.

# Contents

# Introduction

The time has come for young adult ministry to be taken seriously, for practical steps to be made in the direction of new structures and programs for persons between the ages eighteen to thirty-five. The time is ripe, first, because many churches have small percentages of young adults in their congregations. Though an increase of young adults is seen as a crucial goal in many of these churches, the pastors and church members often are heard repeating the common question: "How do we begin to relate with young adults in meaningful ways?" The concern is there; the will is there; but there still remains some doubt about how to proceed and about what is needed for the development of a worthwhile program. The time is ripe, secondly, because there is a great deal of misunderstanding and confusion harbored by young adults and by church leaders concerning each other. On the one hand, young adults sometimes raise cries of resentment toward the church because they feel excluded from meaningful input and participation within the life of the congregation. On the other hand, the church sometimes fails to hear these concerns expressed or does not take them seriously, and it wrestles daily with the question of how a ministry based for so long on a nuclear family model can relate with a group of people who are in many cases "single." All of these factors have resulted in an alliance between young adults and the church which is sometimes close, many times distant, and often absent.

This book is designed to help those who desire to establish and build a new organizational structure and program for young adult ministry, and those who wish to bring a fresh approach and unique ideas to existing ministries. It will present guidelines for organizational structure, including information about in-house church groups, community-based coffee houses and specialized forms of ministry. It will look at different approaches to programming, discussing both evangelical and nonevangelical paths; models of several different kinds of ministries will be used as examples. There is a full chapter on funding for support of programs which will demand a new funding base in order to begin or to be maintained. A complete listing of numerous and diverse resources is also provided in a separate chapter. Thus, the book is meant to be helpful to anyone who is now or will be soon working in the area of young adult ministry. It should provide answers to the puzzling questions, direction to the confusion, and most importantly, a ministry with those who are not now within our reach.

Based mostly upon personal experience in working with young adults in three pastorates and more recently in a coffee-house ministry, the material is drawn from a broad range of life situations in America: the well-to-do, the poor; the educated, the not-so-well-educated; the black church, the white church; those who cope well with life issues and those who do not. While all of these experiences have been meaningful and helpful as background for this writing, it is fair to say that my experience as Director of the Park Avenue Project, an adult programmatic coffee house in Rochester, New York, has provided the primary stimulation and impetus for this work. My interest has grown through watching a small, almost insignificant ministry develop into a larger, more effective and more comprehensive ministry; by hearing people share ideas honestly and openly to the point of helping one another through difficult periods; by feeling the many emotions with people as the height, depth, and breadth of their lives have been expressed; by touching the core of many persons as they have become involved and entwined in the "family" of the Park Avenue Project. It is because of the privileged experience gained at the Project that there is now a desire to share the joy and the sorrow, the successes and the failures—all in the hope that the best of these experiences may be repeated elsewhere.

By now, you should know if this book is for you. In sum, it is for anyone working in the field of young adult ministry, lay persons or clergy. Do you have an interest in organizing a young adult group in your church? Would you like to see a coffee-house ministry for young adults in your area, sponsored ecumenically? Are you looking for ideas to give new life to an existing young adult program? Then read on. If you have *any* interest in providing a more effective young adult ministry, this book is meant to be an instrumental resource. It will help channel your interest and energy toward a familiar or an entirely new group of young adults, bringing even greater fulfillment and extension to your Christian ministry.

We have a great opportunity before us with young adult ministry. Lives can be touched in a healing, helpful manner. In some cases, the church can become visibly and genuinely involved with a whole new age group. We as workers can gain immeasurably from the new people and experiences which God puts before us.

# 1
# Why Have a
# Young Adult Ministry?

The most basic step to be taken by Christian people who wish to develop a young adult ministry involves a self-examination. Before the learning of practical skills concerning organization, program, and fund raising, persons need first to assess and clarify what their rationale is for involvement. Without such a resolution, the commitments of those providing a ministry will lack both anchor and compass; young adults will lack the good feeling that comes through mutual trust and rapport; and the effect of the ministry will be less than it might have been. At stake is an honest and clear definition of thoughts and feelings about young adult ministry, a probing by Christian individuals and groups which can reveal both their levels of interest and reasons for involvement.

The intent of this first chapter is to provide a means for people to develop a rationale for involvement in young adult ministry, a rationale which will be partly identical with what Christians in other places would accept, and partly unique because of the local setting and the individuals involved. In the bulk of the chapter, there is an attempt to identify reasons why the Christian church needs to be working in this area, with the focus upon concerns and issues which are more or less common to all people of the church. The last two sections are intended to help in the determination of a more specific rationale, one which involves an assessment of the unique setting of one's church and community, and an exploration of the motivation, readiness, and sense of commitment brought to the ministry. Taken together, the rationale of the Christian church, the data of the local church and community, and the dimensions of motivation and commitment will provide individuals and groups with a broad and yet quite distinct grounding for young adult ministry, whether intended by lay persons or by professional clergy.

The rationale for ministry with young adults can merely be identified through this process. Only you as an individual or as a member of a group can ultimately choose the reasons for your involvement. The following pages should help in that process.

## Theological Mandate

Theology is the beginning point in presenting a case for the involvement of the Christian church in young adult ministry, since it is theology which informs the beliefs and actions of church members. In this section, a theological mandate for young adult ministry will be offered with an understanding that the delineated points may not be exactly identical with what others would choose. Regardless of the specific points, however, the assumption herein is that a theological mandate is a significant part of a rationale for young adult ministry.

One of the earliest lessons a child learns in a church school program is that God loves all the people of the world: the rich and the poor, the educated and uneducated, the people of America and the people of other countries and cultures, the young and the old. This is a broad theological statement which pertains to all of humanity, including persons who are in the eighteen to thirty-five age range. It affirms that young adults are within the total panorama of God's love.

Those who are raised in the family and fellowship of the Christian church also learn that as disciples of Christ they are commanded to share the gospel message, to bear witness to God's love, and to reach into the community with compassion and extended arms. Since young adults represent a natural and uniform grouping of persons, ministry to this community is certainly one of the potential ways for a church to extend itself. In these general theological statements concerning God's love and Christian outreach, however, there is no specification of young adults as an imperative focus of ministry. It merely says that young adulthood is a potential arena for ministry.

Discipleship does not offer easy answers with regard to the locus of ministry. While Jesus says to Simon Peter and Andrew, "Follow me, and I will make you fishers of men" (Matthew 4:19), and contemporary Christians respond with a willingness to lay down the nets of their subsistence (at least part of the time) and extend themselves into the care of human souls and the sharing of God's love, each person is still confronted with the question, "Where do I direct my attention?" The problem is in knowing how to translate a general theological statement about the extension of God's love into a specific commitment to work with a designated population.

There are, of course, factors which serve to make young adult ministry very interesting, appealing, and urgent, but the actual involvement of people depends upon their conviction that this is the right arena for their time and talents. The full sense of a theological mandate for young adult ministry can be felt only if people truly resolve that a commitment to this work is their best choice for ministry. They have to know why they wish to become bearers of God's love to this community.

Without choosing to answer this question for every person, I would like to share some of the reasons why I think there is a theological mandate for young adult ministry:

1. Young adulthood is a stage of life which comprises a great deal of exploration. Many different life-styles are tried, values are weighed, and confusion about life goals and direction is widely felt. People are flirting with independence for the first time and attempting to find some foundation for stability. Because of the importance of this stage of life as a questing period and as a bridge to a meaningful life in later adulthood, it would seem that a ministry of presence would be a logical and expected response of God's love. By consciously befriending, sharing, being open to questions, and serving as a touchstone throughout this confusing period of exploration, the Christian church could be involved in the lives of many new persons in significant ways.

2. Some young adults experience more than confusion in the period of early adult development. They find that healthy personal growth is hampered or stalled because of specific problems which create a barrier. Examples of various hindrances include drug dependence, alcoholism, psychological problems, low level of education, lack of training for employment, separation and divorce, and others. A theological mandate would seem to be in order here, since these persons really represent the hurting, the victimized, and the destitute. The conveyance of God's love through a specialized form of assisting ministry would seem to be very appropriate.

3. Many young adults today feel estranged from the Christian church. They call into question not only the sincerity of the church but also the traditional theological foundation upon which the church rests. They choose simply to disregard the church, for the most part because it seems to lack personal meaning and importance. A theological mandate would seem to encourage the initiation of dialogue leading to increased mutual understanding, action which is certainly possible on the part of church members.

4. Some young adults are so distant from the Christian church that they have decided to explore other denominations or religions. For example, the Oriental religions (Zen Buddhism, Sufism, the International Society for Krishna Consciousness, etc.) have attracted a large number of disenchanted young Americans, seemingly because they offer an experience of God which is direct, participatory, and personally felt. Other young adults have been drawn to a variety of cult groups, often because of the appeal of charismatic leadership and the promise of a more mystical experience. However, since cults usually emphasize an entirely new way of perceiving the world and represent a sharp break from the prevailing traditions of a society, persons who become adherents of these groups often receive strange and sometimes bizarre answers to their searching questions. The Christian church needs to respond to this exploration by offering a more participatory religious experience and by clearly and meaningfully conveying the value of a Christian faith perspective.

In summary, a theological mandate for young adult ministry is based upon several points: the love of God for all humanity, the expected conveyance of God's love through discipleship, the explorative and confusing nature of early adult development, the special problems which create barriers to personal growth in young adulthood, and the alienation many young adults experience toward organized religion. It must be understood, however, that no list of reasons, however long, will ever compare with the mandate which is derived from a sense of personal devotion and commitment to young adult ministry. Indeed, it is the personal response dimension which finally makes a mandate real.

## Young Adult Attitudes Toward Organized Religion

A primary reason for deciding to organize a young adult ministry is that such a ministry can begin to change the serious doubts which many young adults have toward organized religion. It is a way of establishing a rapport, a trust level, and a means of sharing that is deeper than a ritualistic "hello." In this section, a presentation will be made of the attitudes of young adults who are either somewhat alienated or completely turned off toward organized religion. Realizing that there are also young adults who are quite excited about their membership and participation in the Christian church, the concentration here is given to those who are alienated because it is this population which will form the most significant base for newly created ministries.

In the 1960s, there was much talk about a new morality which was developing, a morality that was freer, more personal, and less authoritative. Wade Clark Roof, speaking about the new morality, says that "Americans under 35 years of age especially, have been highly influenced by changing values in matters of family and sexual styles, drugs and leisure, attitudes toward authority, and concern over personal self-fulfillment."[1] For some people, these changing attitudes have also affected their views about the church and its impact upon them. Religion, however, has not been the only element of human life which has been affected. Roof maintains that the broad range of "this alienation is shown by the degree to which dropouts from the churches also lack confidence in other institutions."[2] Thus, at least in terms of the new morality, it is fair to say that the alienation of large numbers of young adults from the Christian church is symptomatic of a much wider experience of alienation. In other words, the church is symbolic of a tradition which represents the old values, and it is counted as one of the many institutions which do not allow the new morality to be expressed.

At the Park Avenue Project, an adult programmatic coffee house in Rochester, New York, much of this alienation has been shared in a group experience called the Religious Experiment Seminar. Meeting for two hours on Wednesday evenings over a three-year period, the intent of the group was to provide a non-threatening setting where people could share in an open, honest, and informal interchange concerning religious questions and issues. Part of the uniqueness of the group was its attractiveness to people of different faiths: Christians (Unitarian-Universalists, American Baptists, Catholics, Lutherans, fundamentalists), Jews, agnostics, Zen Buddhists, TM adherents, followers of Bahái, and also those few people without any particular allegiance. With all of this variety of background and perspective brought to the group, there was still much that was found to be held in common by group members. Perhaps the most prevailing mood was an uncomfortableness with organized religion, especially with the practice of religion in which a person was raised. Ranging from displeasure to bitterness, an alienation toward religious institutions was definitely felt. In fact, even those who were then practicing church members were somewhat alienated because of the fact that their church did not provide a unique opportunity for honest sharing as found in the Religious Experiment Seminar.

Those who were dissatisfied with the Christian church offer several points in their case. For the purpose of brevity, the remarks made by members of the Religious Experiment Seminar have been condensed and summarized in the following account. It is important to note that few of the people utilized all of the points to express their feelings of alienation; most people would own only a part of the total summary.

1. The Christian church has not allowed me the opportunity of full *participation* in its life. When young adults have been invited to serve on boards or committees, it has seemed like a token involvement. I and others feel that our suggestions are not taken very seriously, and sometimes not even heard.

2. Church lacks *meaning* for me. The hymns are packed with words that do not speak to the contemporary world. Readings are nearly always from the Bible, giving the impression that no one has been inspired by God to write anything since the canon was formed. Sermons are often boring, and generally are a passive experience. The liturgy is so definite and repetitive that it fails to provide a meaningful channel for worship.

3. The minister comes on as a great *authority,* with the Bible as a grounding for every word. This bothers me because I don't like to be told what to believe or what to value or how to live. These kinds of decisions are personal in nature, and they are made on the basis of one's own experience, informed thoughts and private feelings. Also, the world of morality is much grayer than it is black or white, and this means that each person must look responsibly at the issues and make his or her decision.

4. *Hypocrisy* is what I dislike about the church. While setting themselves up as models of Christian living, and then preaching about how I have to conform to their image, some church members forget that we are all equal at the foot of the cross and that there are moments, unquestionably, when even they fail to live up to their standards. I guess it's the "Look at me, I'm perfect" attitude that really bothers me. Besides this personal dimension, the church as an institution is often heard saying things like: "Christianity is the only way" and "We are the true religion." This attitude I see as entirely wrong because it gives to others a message which says: "We don't love you the way you are" and "We will only love you if you are one of us." I don't think that is what Jesus had in mind.

5. The church has *not* allowed for the development of a *personal* theology. Instead, an official doctrine is proclaimed from the pulpit, and the purpose of the church appears to be the subscription of every member to a specific belief system. In reality, people in the congregation often differ on the minor points of a doctrine of theology, and they need to be assured that their own interpretations are okay. I would be more interested in church if I thought that a real concern and appreciation for personal or experiential theology was manifest.

These expressions of alienation toward organized religion have forced people to make decisions about their religious affiliation, some choosing to experiment with another denomination, another religion, cults, or sects, and others deciding to drop all affiliation and attempt to live with a very private religious perspective.

All of these comments point to the distance that has been created between the Christian church and alienated young adults and illustrate how far the church needs to reach before communication with some lives will ever be achieved.

## A Base for the Future

In the life of any institution, a periodic assessment of resources (physical, financial, and human) is needed in order to project its future. Viewing young adults as a human resource of the Christian church, it is not difficult to imagine what the future holds for individual churches who no longer attract young adults or who refuse to take the risk of reaching out to them. The simple fact is that the Christian church has lived through many generations and centuries because it has always had younger adults attending, participating, and ready to fulfill the duties of leadership. Without this resource, the gradual but eventual closing of many church doors in America is inevitable.

It is already known that young adults are a dwindling base of support within the main-line Christian churches. According to a Gallup Poll in 1976, 42 percent of the adult respondents said they attend church in a typical week.[3] This response amounted to a 2 percent increase of churchgoing among all population groups, up from a repeated 40 percent response on this question between 1971 and 1975. Even with the slight increase of churchgoing in 1976, however, the Gallup Poll analysis states that "those under 30 years of age are less likely to attend than are those 30 and over. . . ."[4] Thus, young adults are shown to have a low church attendance rate even at a time when churchgoing among all population groups appears to have increased.

Another report which indicates that young adults are becoming less significant as a base of support for organized religion is an analysis of stayers and switchers among Catholic and Protestant groups in the mid-seventies.[5] The data illustrate that there are many people who decide to move from the religion in which they were raised, switching to other faiths or to none. For example, while 27 percent of the Lutherans in the study decided to switch, 46 percent of the Presbyterians made a change from their original faith. From all of the switching, the various religious groups fared differently in terms of net gains and losses. The greatest net gains from switching were realized by Congregationalists (+32 percent), Episcopalians (+21 percent), and Sectarians[6] (+22 percent), and the greatest net losses were encountered by Methodists (-15 percent), Presbyterians (-10 percent), and Baptists (-9 percent). Although there were no specific figures reported which break down the activity by young adults, the report does state that "as might be expected, young adults across all groups were more likely to have switched to 'none' and less likely to have switched to other faiths."[7] In other words, at a time when many people are choosing to change their membership from one denomination to another, young adults are more likely to choose a path which takes them away from membership and meaningful participation in organized religion.

These reports are instructive for the Christian church because they point to a phenomenon which may be thought to be happening only in one local church or in the few churches within an individual's scope of awareness. With a recognition that the young adult base of the Christian church is deteriorating, and that this is a phenomenon which affects hundreds of churches throughout many denominations, it is important to consider the consequences of a decision *not* to become involved in young adult ministry. It is important to realize that a younger human base is necessary in local churches and denominations in order for those bodies of believers to have a future of continued ministry.

A base for the future is one part of a rationale for becoming involved in a ministry with young adults. It is a serious concern which bothers any church member who desires to see new life always budding within the congregation. Of course, a decision to work with young adults is no guarantee that church rolls will suddenly swell and that new leadership will be forthcoming. That kind of increase will only come as the church speaks to the minds and hearts of young adults, makes provisions for meaningful participation within the life of the congregation, and truly accepts the new members as brothers and sisters in Christ. Moreover, though the future base is an important concern, the new growth in membership may finally occur only as a by-product of a decision to become selflessly involved in a ministry that reaches out to the community of young adults.

## Involvement of Young Adults in the Life of the Church

After realizing the distance which exists between the Christian church and alienated young adults, it would seem that the next logical step would be to work toward creating an environment within churches which would convey the message: "We welcome young adults here; they can find love, meaning, ways to participate, appreciation for their thoughts and feelings, and encouragement in their pilgrimage." Thus, one of the reasons for church members to become involved in young adult ministry is that this work will enable the church to wrestle with its current form and meaning for others. Through this process, the church will learn how to become more inclusive of young adults.

One of the earliest tasks of both professional and lay church leaders is the matter of consciousness-raising within the congregation. The whole church needs to know how distant some young adults are from its life. An appreciative understanding of young adult beliefs and values needs to be nurtured. A commitment to assess the current practice of the church and to work intently toward the creation of an environment which would be more open and inviting to young adults needs to be shared. Admittedly, this educational process takes time, but it is important that the whole church recognize the need for the effort to relate with young adults.

There are several points which have to be evaluated in the life of the congregation. Most basic, of course, is the question of how many young adults are currently involved in the regular worship and activities. This statistic is best obtained by dividing the membership roll into specific age categories and then computing the percentage of the total membership who are in the age range of eighteen to thirty-five. A figure of 10 percent or less would indicate a poor attendance and participation record by young adults, whereas a 25 percent or greater figure would point to a solid support by this age group.

From top to bottom, the practice of the church needs to be assessed. What is the greeting system? What is the percentage of young adults on major boards and committees? How does this figure compare with the percentage of young adults in the congregation? Are there young adults who are given leadership positions or who serve as spokespersons for the congregation? Is the worship experience meaningful to this age group? Are there discussion groups or support groups which serve to challenge the minds and encourage the expression of young adults? The answers to these questions must be taken seriously. On the basis of this data, the church will then be aware of some of the kinds of changes that will need to be instituted in order to create a more inviting environment. If there are already some young adults within the congregation, the church should definitely include them as part of the assessment team, taking its lead especially from their suggestions. Even so, the need for change suggested by young adults who already attend church may not even approach the feelings of others who are alienated from the church. Some changes may have to be rather basic. The changes which are finally made will almost certainly be in the direction of an environment which is genuinely warm, accepting, open, loving, and caring.

## The Context of Church and Community

Another factor which is important in the development of a rationale for young adult ministry is the unique setting provided by a local church and its surrounding community. Individual churches are like the many patterns of snowflakes; no matter how many you look at, there always seems to be something different and unique about each one. What about your church? How is it unique with respect to resources for young adult ministry? The first obvious concern in an assessment is to determine the actual young adult population within the church. Is it a dynamic and vibrant group, or quiet and somewhat small in size? What is the educational background, income level, and life-style which predominates? What kinds of interests are manifested and what issues have strong appeal or reaction? Does the young adult group in the church appear to have the capability of reaching out and building a rapport with others who might be a potential target population of young adult ministry?

Besides human resources, it is also important to consider the financial condition of the church. For example, does the church have the kind of support needed for what is envisioned in programming with young adults? Does it have the wherewithal to raise the necessary money? Then, too, there is the physical property of the church which must be considered. If there are empty, unused rooms, a gymnasium, an auditorium with a stage, a kitchen and dining area, or some other resource even more unique, imagination has to be used to discover how these resources in the church can be meaningfully managed in a young adult ministry. The total array of resources in the church needs to be known in order to appreciate fully the potential for ministry.

Communities differ as much as churches, but a thorough assessment of a particular neighborhood requires a good deal of time. One of the best sources of community data is found in the *United States Census of Population and Housing,* a wealth of study, analysis, and reporting which is published every ten years and found in many libraries.[8] After determining which census tracts pertain to the geographical area being researched, it is then easy to gather information about these tracts with respect to population, age, sex, race, educational levels, employment status, income, marital status, occupations, home ownership, poverty status, and the like. Besides the census data, it is always helpful to read newspaper and magazine articles which speak about general themes relating to young adulthood or which give direct information about the life of young adults in your community. There might also be special studies done by local government offices or by private groups which help to illuminate the young adult population. Just being observant of young adult patterns in your community will also be helpful: concentrations of residence, favorite pastimes, kinds of life-styles, and obvious needs. All meaningful data which is gathered will help to determine the place, scope, and focus of an intended young adult ministry; it may point in the direction of an apartment-house ministry, a coffee-house ministry, a group at the church for singles, or a support group for single parents. In addition to the ideas presented above, chapter 8 includes a listing of books which go into detail concerning the task of studying one's community. Also, one of the sections in chapter 4 presents ideas about identifying potential community resources which might be utilized in programming with young adults.

The church and community setting out of which each person decides about becoming involved in young adult ministry is crucial. It represents the real world where problems are perceived, resources are joined, and visions of new life are born. It brings a note of practicality to the decision making, because the people who live in each setting *feel* the needs as they experience the life there.

## Motivation, Readiness, and Commitment for Ministry

This last section is summed up in one question: "Are you ready to assume leadership and other responsibilities in a young adult ministry?" It is a very personal question aimed at determining the sense of motivation, capability, and commitment which is brought to the ministry. The answer that each person formulates about his or her readiness for ministry will undoubtedly be an important factor in one's rationale for ministry.

Motivation for working with young adults can be derived from many sources. David might be motivated because of knowing about a twenty-four-year-old woman who experienced loneliness and depression and then decided that suicide was the only answer. Suzanne might get involved because she feels that young adults would be a "fun" age group. Marcy makes her decision on the basis of the gospel, thinking that Jesus is pointing her in the direction of a specific young adult population. Ralph is motivated because he wants to see a night place developed which would be an alternative to bars. In virtually every case, those who desire to work with young adults are motivated by something very specific—the age level, theological concerns, special needs, or something else. It is important for each person to recognize what that motivating factor is.

The question of whether a person is "ready" for ministry is also quite important for consideration. In assuming leadership, people will need to exercise planning, organizational, program, and probably fund-raising skills. For those who wish to involve themselves by befriending others and serving as a touchstone, it will be important to be objective, to empathize, and to know how to refer people to sources of help. Some may come to young adult ministry with additional skills that can be utilized, such as playing a musical instrument, painting, writing funding proposals, or knowing how to organize a drama workshop. The decision about readiness for ministry is a personal one and can only be determined after assessing the requirements of the situation and the strengths brought to it. If you are not completely sure about your readiness, be assured that your involvement will teach you many of the skills that are needed. Chapters 3, 4, and 5 are intended to be instructive in this area as well.

Commitment for ministry refers to tenacity, stick-to-it-iveness, follow-through, and seriousness in wanting to see new life brought about. It means that the original purpose is far too important to be interrupted or halted on the basis of personality problems or conflict over program management. Commitment, following upon motivation and an assessment of readiness, is the one very crucial factor which will have the most significant effect upon whether a young adult ministry succeeds in its intended purpose and is able to be maintained.

## Conclusion

A rationale for young adult ministry should not be confused with a statement of concern, because the latter is often nothing more than an assent to a potential course of action. Church organizations are especially famous for stating approvals of concern and authorization of action by their constituents, without gaining the commitments of people actually to become concerned. Instead, a rationale for young adult ministry is rooted in a sense of definite preparation for action. It is formulated as a sound and functional grounding for commitment. All of the elements of a rationale for young adult ministry give credence to a person's involvement and heighten the motivation and purpose for the ministry. The development of a rationale is a worthy exercise for all persons contemplating such a ministry, whether this is done individually, as members of a group, or as participants in a large body of believers. What is finally formulated will be unique in each case and will illustrate very clearly why people want to work with young adults.

# 2
# The Young Adult

Now that a rationale for young adult ministry has been fully probed and developed, each person who is about to begin such a ministry should be able to say: "I know that young adult ministry is for me; this is what God is saying to me; this is what my thoughts and feelings say; and this is where my sense of commitment is pointing." Indeed, this is an important statement because it allows for personal ownership of one's work and provides a positive foundation for involvement with young adults. The rationale, however, is only part of the foundation needed for this particular area of ministry. In addition, those who desire to work with young adults must have a full comprehension of the various characteristics which would describe the fifty-seven million persons in America who are within the eighteen to thirty-five age range. With such a preparation, a person's foundation for young adult ministry will be broadened to include many important and relevant perceptions of early adulthood. Thus, the intention of this chapter is to provide a descriptive account of the young adult.

## Early Adult Development

Until only a few years ago, the human life cycle was understood in terms of a simple progression: infancy, childhood, adolescence, and then adulthood. Much research and writing had been done about people who were eighteen and younger, but very little understanding was offered about what people experienced in adulthood. Perhaps this was so because people believed so strongly that the passing from adolescence to adulthood signified maturity, stability, and responsibility, and therefore all of the attention of research was devoted to the stages prior to adulthood to insure that more was known about these transitional stages.

Thanks to recent research and reporting by persons like Gail Sheehy, the entire human life cycle can now be appreciated for its numerous identifiable stages.[1] Adulthood is no longer considered one unit of time where maturity is realized; instead, it is several units of time or passages which are distinguishable from one another by the experiences, problems, and crises characteristic of each period. Since there are potential crises in each of the several stages of adulthood, this means that adults, too, are continually growing and always refining their ability to cope with new life experiences.

Early adulthood is but one period of the human life cycle, a brief span of approximately eighteen years. Nonetheless, within this period of time, there are now a number of stages or passages which can be identified. Distinguishable from one another on the basis of predictable crises and typical human experiences, these stages illustrate very clearly that the factors of age and human development can greatly determine the potential focus for ministry with a young adult population.

"Pulling up roots" is the first stage of early adulthood; Gail Sheehy says that after the age of eighteen "college, military service, and short-term travels are all customary vehicles our society provides for the first round trips between family and a base of one's own."[2] She further says:

> The tasks of this passage are to locate ourselves in a peer group role, a sex role, an anticipated occupation, an ideology or world view. As a result, we gather the impetus to leave home physically and the identity to *begin* leaving home emotionally.[3]

After pulling up roots, young adults experience a passage which is labeled "the trying twenties":

> Our focus shifts from the interior turmoils of late adolescence—"Who am I?" "What is truth?"—and we become almost totally preoccupied with working out the externals. "How do I put my aspirations into effect?" "What is the best way to start?" "Where do I go?" "Who can help me?" "How did *you* do it?"
>
> In this period, which is longer and more stable compared with the passage that leads to it, the tasks are as enormous as they are exhilarating: To shape a Dream, that vision of ourselves which will generate energy, aliveness, and hope. To prepare for a lifework. To find a mentor if possible.

And to form the capacity for intimacy, without losing in the process whatever consistency of self we have thus far mustered. The first test structure must be erected around the life we choose to try.[4]

Thus, the period of the trying twenties incorporates much exploration, decision making, and concern in the attempt to begin building a foundation which will be stable into the future; however, it also appears to involve an underlying young adult fear that "the choices we make are irrevocable."[5] Challenging the latter assumption, Sheehy maintains that "change is quite possible, and some alteration of our original choices is probably inevitable."[6] With all of the exploring that does go on during this period, it is interesting to note that much of this happens out of a sense of obligation. According to Sheehy, the most pervasive theme of the trying twenties is "doing what we *'should,'*" and "the 'shoulds' are largely defined by family models, the press of the culture, or the prejudices of our peers."[7]

The next stage is named "catch-30," a time when people become impatient with devoting themselves to the "shoulds," when "important new choices must be made, and commitments altered or deepened."[8] Tearing up the life which was pieced together in the twenties is a common response of people experiencing catch-30:

> It may mean striking out on a secondary road toward a new vision or converting a dream of "running for president" into a more realistic goal. The single person feels a push to find a partner. The woman who was previously content at home with children chafes to venture into the world. The childless couple reconsiders children. And almost everyone who is married, especially those married for seven years, feels a discontent.[9]

The self takes on greater value during catch-30, with both men and women becoming concerned about how they can improve themselves—in their occupations, in their formal education, in the learning of practical skills. Newly felt needs of the self are often in conflict in the lives of married couples, and this can be a definite source of discontent.

After catch-30, Gail Sheehy asserts that young adults undergo a period of "rooting and extending":

> Life becomes less provisional, more rational and orderly in the early thirties. We begin to settle down in the full sense. Most of us begin putting down roots and sending out new shoots. People buy houses and become very earnest about climbing career ladders. Men in particular concern themselves with "making it." Satisfaction with marriage generally goes

downhill in the thirties (for those who have remained together) compared with the highly valued, vision-supporting marriage of the twenties. This coincides with the couple's reduced social life outside the family and the in-turned focus on raising their children.[10]

At the age of thirty-five, when early adulthood comes to an end, people enter a period called "the deadline decade." It is a difficult passage because it involves "the loss of youth, the faltering of physical powers we have always taken for granted, the fading purpose of stereotyped roles by which we have thus far identified ourselves, [and] the spiritual dilemma of having no absolute answers. . . ."[11]

In summary, young adults pass through a number of stages in the experience of early adult development. Those who work in young adult ministry need to be aware of the passages of early adult development and conscious of the necessity to tailor a ministry to the specific needs related to human experience.

## Characteristics of Young Adults

Young adults in any period of time will be influenced by a variety of factors: historical events, societal norms, contemporary culture patterns, family expectations, and so forth. Because of the changing nature of elements such as history, norms, culture patterns, and family influence, each generation of young adults will have particular modes of behavior, cherished ideas, and chosen values. While all members of a specific generation cannot be easily described with the use of one set of characteristics, it is often true that generalities can be drawn about a majority of persons. With this in mind, several observed characteristics of present-day young adults will now be discussed. In order to highlight these characteristics, there will be comparisons made with the behavior patterns and values of those who were young adults just a few years ago. Most of what is presented has been learned through meeting and talking with many persons in a variety of ministry settings.

The first characteristic that helps to describe young adults today is the emphasis upon introspection and the self instead of social action. While the Vietnam War held the attention of thousands of young adults in the 1960s, with people organizing in marches, protests, and individualized forms of public dissent, contemporary young adults are looking inward, attempting to discover who they are and how they can intensify the experience of self. The interest in astrology, therapy, family roots, transcendental meditation, hobbies, the single life, and childless marriages is some indication that there is a major concern today with the self. Because of this pronounced interest, many people have been able to experience a kind of personal growth and self-knowledge that may never have been possible in another period of history. Of course, it is also unfortunately true that some people have taken this interest to such an extreme that they have neglected to develop a concern for others.

A second shift has to do with suspicion and distrust of authority. A number of people today no longer seem to grant their respect to formerly standard representatives of authority, for example, the police, the clergy, politicians, city officials, and members of the health professions. Instead, many young adults are heard saying that respect must be earned by living and acting in a fair, respectable, and responsible manner. I remember that when I first became director of the Park Avenue Project, there were people who were quite suspicious of me. Though the Project is labeled as a nonevangelical form of young adult ministry, still there were participants who wondered when I was going to pull the Bible out of my back pocket and begin preaching. Because I did not do that, and attempted to relate honestly as a person rather than as a professional clergyman, a good rapport with mutual trust developed, and a foundation for potential ministry was established.

Another recognizable characteristic embodied in today's young adults is a greater latitude of exploration. First of all, more time is taken today for exploration; it is not inconceivable for people to exhaust most of the trying twenties by searching, exploring, and experiencing what life can offer. Then, too, there are more options which are tried today—different life-styles, sexual preferences, a variety of belief systems, the world of drugs, a wide range of acceptable values, assorted fads, contrasting ideas about work, and the like. Because of these numerous choices, the latitude of exploration is broadened. Moreover, while there tends to be a great deal of questioning, searching, and experimenting, many young adults nevertheless remain indecisive concerning available options. Since this uncertainty often persists, some people constantly feel the necessity of looking further, and therefore the latitude of exploration is extended again and again.

A fourth shift has been in the area of the degree of commitment in relationships. Many young adults today simply do not look forward to marriage, resolving instead to maintain a single existence while perpetually dating one person after another, or choosing to contract with individuals concerning living arrangements for various durations of time. Single living is experienced in America by at least half of the fifty-seven million persons in early adulthood. This pattern of living tends to disallow any manifestation of lifelong or permanent commitment in relationships. It allows instead for an open door of freedom at times when friends and mates become too restrictive, tiring, or abusive. Noncommittal relationships are also evident in the marriages which by choice do not want children. While there are many reasons given for this choice, such as the idea that the world as it is does not need more children, one of the primary reasons for choosing not to bear and raise children is often because the demand of time, energy, and money is considered to be so great. Thinking that the world can be experienced more richly as an individual who is not restricted, some young adults have chosen to refrain from making a commitment in relationship with children.

The fifth and last shift is documented in *The General Mills American Family Report, 1976-77: Raising Children in a Changing Society*.[12] Discussing how the twenty-three million American families with children under thirteen years of age are coping with the problems of raising their children in a period of rapid social change, the report concludes that parents can now be classified as "Traditionalists" or as members of the "New Breed." Traditionalists, who represent 57 percent of all parents of children under thirteen years of age, value marriage as an institution, religion, saving money, hard work, and financial security.[13] Traditional parents

are child-oriented (ready to sacrifice for their children); they want their children to be outstanding; want to make decisions for their children; respect authority; are not permissive with their children; believe boys and girls should be raised differently; and see having children as a very important value.[14]

New Breed parents (43 percent) "have rejected many of the traditional values by which they were raised: marriage as an institution, the importance of religion, saving and thrift, patriotism and hard work for its own sake."[15] New Breed parents

are self-oriented (not ready to sacrifice for their children), don't push their children, feel that children should be free to make their own decisions, question authority, are permissive with their children, believe boys and girls should be raised alike, believe their children have no future obligation to them, and see having children as an option, not a social responsibility.[16]

And while the Traditionalists and the New Breed parents are clearly different in what they value, they nevertheless choose to teach a few identical values to their children: duty before pleasure, my country right or wrong, hard work pays off, people in authority know best, and sex is wrong without marriage.[17] It is especially interesting that the New Breed parents resolve to make value accommodations for their children, while maintaining a somewhat different set of values for themselves; for example, notice the different positions about authority and marriage.

Though these observed characteristics are probably not representative of every young adult in American society, they are nevertheless recognizable in large segments of the young adult population. The parent classifications of Traditionalist and New Breed used in the General Mills Report might also be helpful in describing young adults in general, since some people tend to adhere to the old values and some want to proclaim the new. However, because young adulthood is such a fluid and confusing time, it is probably also true that some individuals are partly Traditionalist and partly the New Breed at the same time.

## A Synopsis of the Self

One of the most interesting and meaningful groups at the Park Avenue Project is the Human Relations Workshop, which gathers every week to discuss concerns and questions about personal and relational human issues. At the beginning of each series, people who become involved in the early planning sessions begin to choose possible themes for discussion. Since the finally planned schedule is always the creation of a group of young adults who take the responsibility for planning, it would seem that a studied glance at the topics of several series would indicate some of the important life issues which are of major concern to a large number of young adults.

Looking at ten different schedules of the Human Relations Workshop, offered between January, 1976, and April, 1979, the most striking impression is that nearly all of the many weekly topics are concerned with some aspect of the self. While each series has been well mixed with a wide range of topics, it is nonetheless true that 95 percent of the topics can be placed in one of eight different categories of the self. These categories will be presented in the following pages.

## 1. The Agitated Self

There have been group discussions on doubts, fears, loneliness, anxiety, and depression. Usually, people have wanted to check their own experience against others, hoping to feel okay about the feelings which they have experienced. The group has often responded to these issues by offering ideas about how people might begin to deal with the feelings and situations they face.

## 2. The Self in Control

Many people have been concerned with the ability to be in control of their lives instead of feeling that they are helpless, passive victims of life's experience. As examples of this concern, themes have been covered which deal with shaping the future, facing social pressures, budgeting money-time-food-energy, confronting everyday annoyances, overcoming the temptation of drug use, building community, resolving conflicts, being aware of feelings, and being able to express emotions. Gaining control over one's life is definitely an important theme within the age span of young adulthood.

## 3. The Self Understood

People have earnestly searched for a formal, studied understanding of the self, through discussions about ego states and transactions, life scripts, the self-concept, human capability and changeability, and the normal self in comparison with extreme personality types. The concern here is to learn about the self in a more analytical sense, by asking questions, such as "What is the self?" and "How is a personality defined and described?"

## 4. The Growing Self

Young adults are naturally concerned about the direction of their own growth and development. The Human Relations Workshop has provided opportunities for discussing assertiveness, personal integration, the transitions of adult life, maintenance of mental health, the effect of early environment on adulthood, and sources of inner strength, beliefs, and values. People want to be sure that they are maintaining a healthy outlook and balance in life, and that some growth is occurring.

## 5. The Shared Self

One of the most important issues in the group experience has been the self in relation with others. How do I reach out? What does it feel like to have a genuine friendship? When is intimacy appropriate?

These kinds of questions have been asked during sessions which have dealt with the ethics of intimacy, problems in relationships, different life-styles, friendship and betrayal, modern meanings of marriage, commitment in relationships, divorce, getting beyond stereotyping, and difficulties in communicating. Since young adulthood is the first time when many people begin to live independently and relate with others on their own terms, it is logical that much confusion and concern would arise about the self in relation with others. It is a persistent theme.

### 6. The Sexual Self

Discussion in this area has always attracted a large number of participants. It is a popular theme for discussion because it is of deep concern to many people. In the workshop, people have discussed sex roles and stereotypes, life as a woman, sexual expectations, and myths. An entire series on human sexuality was planned for the spring of 1978, covering physiology and sexual identity, options for sexual expression, common psychosexual problems, sexual ethics, and relationships. The sexual self is a theme of great importance in young adulthood.

### 7. The Working Self

Interest in this area has been focused upon the pressures of the workaday world, the meaning of work, the relationship of education and employment, and career options. Because work is generally a mandatory task for existence, the concern of most people has been that their work be at least somewhat enjoyable. Those who do fully enjoy their work have been considered very fortunate by the other members of the group.

### 8. The Final Self

Even at young ages, there is some concern about death and grief. People have desired to compare their own feelings and experiences with those of others.

These themes of the self or life issues are certainly not exhaustive of what young adults are thinking and caring about, but they do indicate some specific concerns of persons in this age span. They function as a window into the inner thoughts and feelings of one sample of young adults. Religion as a life issue has not been covered in this section because religious discussion is almost always done by other groups at the Park Avenue Project—the Religious Experiment and the Cosmic Dimension. Discussion of these group experiences is reserved for a later section of this chapter.

## A Horizontal System of Support

One of the most essential points to understand about young adults is that they want to be respected as persons of value, and they want to feel that they are worthy of the trust of others. If a young adult ministry does not realize this from the beginning and instead approaches the tasks of ministry with the object of saving the despicable and the unlovely, and trusting the people only after special conditions have been met, the result will be that many young adults will not feel respected, appreciated, and wanted. Basic to the development of Christian ministry with young adults is a respect for persons and a trust of their integrity. This is the first element of a horizontal system of support for young adults.

Also, young adults strongly desire to participate in and at least partially to control their own process. This means that the planning of young adult activities must involve young adults in that exercise. The leadership of programs must include young adults. The entire young adult ministry must allow people to participate meaningfully, which means that decision making must be largely if not wholly in their hands. A church cannot maintain a meaningful young adult ministry if it controls the activities of the participants, brings judgment upon people for their interests, or slaps the hands of young adults in a paternal or maternal fashion. A ministry must convey the message that participants are going to be treated as equals, as brothers and sisters, as people of worth, and as children of God.

Another way of speaking with regard to a horizontal system of support is the fact that young adults do not appreciate a ministry that is *to* them or *for* them, but instead one which is *with* them. Very few people care for a model of ministry which is condescending or which gives them the impression that they are worthless. Neither do people care for models of ministry which are prepackaged and totally decided by others. A ministry *with* young adults is one which says "I'm *with* you"; "I *respect* you"; "I *trust* you"; "I'm *present*"; "I *care* enough to want to be your *friend*"; "I *love* you *unconditionally.*" It is a ministry which looks straight ahead at people, reaches out with an extended hand, and rejoices in the mutual sharing which results.

These are simple points but still very essential to the whole fabric of ministry. They are focused upon the concepts of attitude, intention, and approach of ministry. With careful attention to how a ministry is begun with young adults—with respect, trust, meaningful participation, control of the process, and an attitude that says "I am *with* you"—a young adult ministry will have a great chance to grow and to flourish. The horizontal system of support, from one human being to another, is an extremely important consideration in the building of a young adult ministry.

## The Matter of Faith

In all of the nights that the Religious Experiment and Cosmic Dimension groups have met at the Park Avenue Project, and with all of the attraction those groups sometimes have had to people who are confused about or seriously searching the meaning of their religious beliefs, I have never met a participant who was ready to say: "I do not believe in God," or "I have no trust in life." People have offered a wide variety of concepts about God, some of which are fairly traditional and some unconventional, but no one has entertained the belief that God is not a part of human experience. Religious questions, issues, and beliefs are of real concern to young adults, even if many may find it difficult to accept totally a traditional doctrine as espoused by members of the Christian faith. Perhaps a presentation of a few representative belief systems from members of these two groups will help to illustrate the matter of faith as it is conceived by some young adults.

The first belief system I would mention is *Christian Tradition*. People who have affirmed the tradition of a specific church or denomination have usually been members of those bodies. They have often had no difficulty accepting the literal meaning of the Apostles' Creed, the physical resurrection of Jesus, the idea that Jesus is the Incarnate Word, and the belief that the Holy Bible is the Word of God. While a few people might quibble over some of the finer points of these beliefs, they still have been willing, essentially, to accept and to own the belief system.

A second example of what people believe might be called *Christian Humanism*. Proponents of this view say that Jesus was a real human being just like anyone else, but that he responded to God in a way which had never been done. He became special to the people of his times and to those in later times because of the seriousness, uniqueness, and effectiveness of his ministry. This belief system favors a spiritual resurrection and the thoughtful translation of church doctrine and the words of the Bible into meaningful terms. It maintains that because of the model of Jesus, all of humanity now has the evidence that a genuine response to God is possible, as well as the hope that this will be effected more and more in human lives. Jesus is the proof that life has promise, and it is he alone who provides the model for this belief system.

The next belief system might be referred to as *Plural Prophets.* People who hold to this position affirm that God has chosen to make a message known to the world through many human beings. Jesus is an extremely important example of those through whom God has spoken, but he is only one example. Buddha, Confucius, and Muhammad would be other leaders of religious movements who would be considered in the same way. Some of the proponents of this plural prophets' viewpoint would also include more contemporary people, such as Dr. Martin Luther King, Jr., or Mahatma Gandhi. The important point here is that people believe that God has not chosen to restrict the number of prophets or incarnations in the past and will not be expected to do so in the future. We are encouraged to look at all of life and to hold precious those words, examples, and experiences which we believe God has given to us.

*Experiential Theology* is another belief system, and this focuses upon the personal and private religious experience of the individual. While some of its advocates might also belong to a church or synagogue, or believe that certain prophets in the history of the world have been expressive of God's will, this belief system is centered upon the idea that "What is important in the matter of faith is what God is saying to me right now, in the present, through my experience." In other words, the most crucial information a person can receive about the nature and practice of faith is discovered in the day-to-day communications and learnings with God and in the affirmations for living and ministering which are rooted in personal experience.

A final example is that of *Reincarnation,* a belief system which holds that the essence of people (the soul) never dies. It maintains that upon the bodily death of a person the soul might be given additional opportunities to continue living, but in another bodily form. This can lead to some interesting discussions about the question of a limited number of souls in the universe or about the thought of a soul first being in a human and then, for example, in a chicken. Proponents of reincarnation basically say that it is possible for some souls to receive many opportunities to continue living in some bodily form, and these are for the soul's potential improvement in learning the art and practice of living.

These, then, are five examples of how some young adults conceive their religious belief systems. Though other people have entertained more individual and somewhat abnormal beliefs, such as concluding that UFOs are really angels trying to communicate with us, the five examples provide the most common categories of belief systems for people who have attended these groups. Those who adhere to these various expressions are serious about their religion, even if they are still searching for clearer or more meaningful answers to their questions. The matter of faith is thus very important to young adults, at a time when many persons, at least for the present, cannot wholly identify with organized religion.

## Conclusion

Finally, it must also be said that every human being is quite unique and, to an extent, defies general description. Each of us has a distinctive background, experience, current situation, set of interests, abilities, and personality. One young adult might be a black thirty-year-old bank manager who is single by choice, a Christian Humanist, an apartment dweller, a photographic hobbyist, and also a person who thrives on finding time for herself. Another young adult might be a white twenty-three-year-old folk singer who believes in Plural Prophets, enjoys reading about Sherlock Holmes, remains confused about women after his third divorce, lives in a rooming house, and associates with people only irregularly. The actual people who will comprise a young adult ministry will be so unique that no descriptive account in general terms can ever hope to depict fully their lives.

Even so, an appreciation of the general characteristics which are noticeable within the young adult population in America is important in the development of a broad and comprehensive understanding of people in the early adult years. Along with the formulation of a rationale for ministry (chapter 1), this descriptive account serves as an important foundation in preparation for working with young adults.

# 3
# Guidelines for Organizational Structure

Essential to the movement of the human body is the skeletal structure, a strong and durable framework which provides form and flexibility for the management of many physical functions. In much the same way, a young adult ministry requires a framework or organizational structure. Formed out of many connected components, an organizational structure for ministry includes elements such as a statement of purpose, a place for ministry, a governing board, leadership, an operational code, goals and objectives, and a human support base. These several elements provide a structure out of which ministry can happen. They give form, enable movement, and establish support for the many needed functions related to young adult ministry.

When a new ministry is seriously envisioned, consideration of practical steps of how to begin must soon follow. This chapter is intended to provide guidelines for people who wish to develop an organizational structure which is both suitable and sound for their own situations. While the subject matter in the following pages may seem unimportant to some people, that is really not the case; the following material represents fundamental and significant considerations for the building of a young adult ministry. If there is any hope of designing a ministry which will have the potential of lasting through time, involving young adults on a participatory level, and confronting many problematic situations, then an appreciation of the vital components of an organizational structure is certainly in order.

## Initiation

Some people look at caterpillars and contemplate the fragile, long, and wiggly body which is before them; then there are others who look at caterpillars and envision their potential—the light and beautifully colored form of the butterfly. In much the same way, members of the Christian community observe a young adult population and experience differences of perception. Some see the young adults in a very descriptive manner, thinking of their habits and characteristics. But then there are others who not only see the young adults but also envision what their potential lives might be if a ministry was organized to work with them. They are able to imagine the changes, the growth, and the increase which are all possibilities of the present. These people who are able to "envision" are very important in the development of a young adult ministry, for this is the first step in the process of initiation.

At some point, what is envisioned must be brought to the attention of an official group: a committee, the church board, or a larger church organization. The conceptualized ministry needs to be shared in order to be considered seriously for support and adoption by a church membership. Of course, this task of presenting is not an easy one for all people. The human mind is often very quick to think of reasons why the suggestion might be viewed as foolish, unusual, or ridiculous; also, in appraising the known feelings of those who sit on these boards and committees, the potential for resistance and denial of support may sometimes be exaggerated. An attempt must be made to overcome these thoughts and instead to approach the task of presenting with a hopeful and positive attitude. As long as the presentation is done well, with feeling, and with full explanation of what is being proposed, there is always the possibility that the vision of the presenter will be confirmed by others in the group.

What is proposed might be a ministry to relate with runaways— late teens who have decided to break away from the family mold. Temporary housing in the homes of church members could be one of the negotiated terms of such a ministry. Another proposal might be in the direction of expansion of a current young adult group in a church. Suggestions could come in the form of supplementary program possibilities, new ways of evangelization, specific procedures for jointly programming with other established young adult groups, or ideas for increasing the utilization of the church building by young adults, including the worship area. Still another proposal might offer the recommendation that the church assist a group of young adults in starting a coffee house in the community. In this case, church space could be requested, or money for initial equipment, such as coffee urns, tables, and chairs. What is proposed in each church meeting will be quite distinctive, but the ideas in all cases must be clearly stated in terms of what is envisioned as ministry, what is suggested as the church's involvement, and what is specifically requested in the way of assistance. People will want to know the proposed place of ministry, the purpose, the anticipated leadership, the potential support base, and the expected term of the ministry. In other words, a great deal of preparation has to be given to the task of presenting.

Even after a young adult ministry is endorsed, careful attention must be given to the process of feedback and reporting. There should be a system whereby the church membership is constantly informed and educated about the ministry. In this way, what is envisioned, presented, and endorsed will become even further appreciated by the sponsoring church organization.

## Statement of Purpose

A statement of purpose is a broad and general declaration of intent formulated by newly started groups and organizations. Composed in the form of a paragraph or a list of several points, the statement of purpose is a way of clearly defining the general parameters of interest in the establishment of a young adult ministry. People who especially need to participate in the drafting of such a statement are the clergy and lay leaders who are organizing the ministry, representatives of the young adult population, and those who are offering substantial financial support and commitment. What is drafted will have to satisfy everyone concerned, for it will always be referred to as the general guideline for understanding and promoting the nature of the ministry.

When the Park Avenue Project was organized in June, 1974, by Immanuel Baptist Church in Rochester, New York, the statement of purpose affirmed by the church was summed up in a general and open phrase, namely, "to relate with young adults in meaningful ways." Designed in terms of a secular coffee-house style of ministry, the Project soon began to attract many young adults, who then assumed responsibility for expanding upon the original statement of purpose by specifying a number of general programmatic directions. Examples of these additionally developed points are: "to provide a warm, accepting, nonthreatening, and homelike atmosphere," "to organize a variety of interest groups according to needs," "to offer counseling/referral," "to provide unique volunteer opportunities." Thus, in the case of the Park Avenue Project, there were really two draftings contributing to the final design of a statement of purpose, one that was quite general and open, and another that was more specific with regard to programmatic intent, developed by the people who were actually involved in the response of ministry.

A more evangelical form of proposed ministry would naturally state a different emphasis. Examples of general points which might appear in a statement of purpose include the following: "to share the gospel message of love as known through the life of Jesus," "to liberate the captives from the world of drugs, prostitution, and degradation," "to bring the peace of Christ into the lives of people who are experiencing the confusing period of early adult development," or "to offer wholeness through a ministry of presence." Since the theology of those who are designing various young adult ministries will differ, the statements of purpose of these groups will be written in a phrasing that is familiar and distinctive in each case. Regardless of particular emphasis, however, the important point is that a statement of purpose is an opportunity for those who are organizing a young adult ministry to determine in a general way the parameters and the focus of the intended ministry. The inclusion of young adults in this process from the very beginning is absolutely crucial to the hope of having people identify with the purpose and desire to participate fully in the programming.

One of the more controversial subjects relating to a statement of purpose is the question of whether the proposed ministry is expected to produce an increase in church membership. If this is indeed the expectation, then it really should be honestly stated from the beginning and made clear along with the other points in the purpose statement. If the ministry is more secular in nature, and the church is willing to reach out with an accepting love and without any firm expectations with regard to church membership, then this mood of the church also needs to be stated honestly. Honesty and clarity in all cases are necessary in order to lay all of the agendas on the table and provide an atmosphere of trust.

## Building Usage

Unless a ministry is totally designated to operate "in the street," "in the marketplace," or in some other free and open area, those who are organizing a young adult ministry will have to consider the question of a meeting place which can be utilized. Of course, the nature and scope of the ministry will to a large extent determine spatial needs. A single parents' group which meets weekly for discussion might be able to function with a room in the church or with a rotation of meetings in different group members' homes. A group of singles in their late teens might want to have a place within the church for which they can take full responsibility—being free to decorate and to furnish according to the wishes of the group. An apartment house ministry might require nothing more than access to the building and a responsible deportment while there, since much of the ministry can be geared to happen within individual apartments. A coffee-house ministry might demand a permanent place in a church or community building which can be used solely for that purpose, or it may have to compromise by agreeing to set up and tear down props each time the place is used. One of the first tasks in organizing a young adult ministry then is to determine clearly specific spatial needs and to work toward finding suitable areas for use.

Having group responsibility for a particular space, whether this be a room in the church, a converted basement, or an unused parsonage of the church, is a valuable idea for young adult ministry because it allows for the feeling of ownership. Citing the Park Avenue Project as an example, the program is located on the first floor of a large Tudor house which was once the parsonage of Immanuel Baptist Church. People who attend the Project have painted the rooms, donated the furniture, cleaned, installed storm windows, mowed the lawn, cared for a garden, shoveled snow, and done many other jobs relating to the physical property. Because of this involvement and investment of energy, the sense of group ownership of the program is very high. In fact, the results have been so positive that I would encourage the same kind of property management agreement between other young adult programs and their sponsors.

Most young adult ministries will probably be located in properties that are not legally owned by the participants of the young adult groups. This means that a tenant-landlord relationship will usually be formed, an affinity that is sometimes congenial and sometimes rather discordant. It is important to recognize the fragile moorings of any space which is donated or rented and to realize the necessity of a sincere attempt to act responsibly in the use of any such property. The way in which church or community property is used, maintained, and improved will have an effect upon the continuation of a relationship, the attitudes people develop about young adults, and the sense of ownership and responsibility engendered within a young adult group.

Having a space is an important consideration in the development of a young adult ministry, since it can foster a feeling of group cohesion, a notion of self-sufficiency and ownership, and a sense of confidence about continuity. Because the use of a building is often a gift and at the discretion of others, it will behoove those who serve as tenants to appreciate the opportunity of building usage and to show that the good care and management of the physical property are mutually important.

## Governing Board

A governing board is a vital part of the organizational structure for young adult ministry. Its value is appreciated in what it provides: order, representation, direction, and accountability. It is through the governing board that business is handled, major policy decisions are made, responses to potential problems are jointly determined, programs are evaluated, new sources of funds are researched and considered, and a state-of-the-budget message is supplied at periodic intervals. Though many people will be heard complaining about the number of board meetings they have to attend, most still appreciate the fact that a governing board is one of the best available means of managing an organization. It is an element of organizational structure which is absolutely basic, and which will likely be for many years to come.

In establishing a governing board, the first logical questions will concern membership. Who will sit on the board? Who should rightfully have a voice if not a vote? Who will be able to give effective leadership to the organization? People who might be considered include those interested young adults who want to relate in some way with a new ministry, church members who represent various church boards and committees, community residents who strongly identify with the ministry and offer special skills, the clergy and/or lay leadership of a proposed ministry, and representatives of church organizations and agencies which are contributing substantial support.

The way in which boards are first organized follows a typical pattern. People gather on the basis of shared interests, agree to a statement of purpose, express a need for a structure of some kind, and establish board membership by vote. In thinking about specific persons who might be asked to serve on a board, it will be important to consider the issue of representation and also whether people have the capability for leadership, decision making, and the exercising of valuable skills. Fund-raising experience, ability to chair a meeting, and knowledge of legal questions are some of the strengths which might be sought. However, if only a few people with special skills are available and many others are eager to serve, willing to learn, and absolutely committed to the ministry, the governing board will still have a good beginning.

Some governing boards are loosely structured while others are more formally organized; these differences are usually obvious from a reading of the bylaws or charters of various organizations. The bylaws are the procedures by which an organized group agrees to operate, establishing a set order with regard to officers, elections, duties, regularity of meetings, and like matters. The specific duties of board members may differ somewhat from one board to another, and the procedures for business may vary, but governing boards will usually consist of the same basic elements. For those who wish to explore the various elements which are normally considered in the establishment of bylaws, a reading of sections of *Robert's Rules of Order* would be helpful.[1]

The governing board of each organization is really quite unique because of the specific people who are represented and also the way the members have chosen to conduct their meetings. Some boards are open, informal, and cheerful, while others are formal and solemn, but all are important instruments in the regular handling of business and in the provision of a supportive structure for ministry. The governing board for young adult ministry might be established as one of the primary boards of a local church or as one of the boards of a local denominational or ecumenical group. It may also choose to stand on its own through a separately incorporated status.

## Leadership

One of the questions invariably raised with respect to leadership is whether a voluntary staff is sufficient to conduct a young adult ministry. The other choice is a paid staff, and everyone knows what that means in terms of budgeting requirements. Perhaps the experience of the Park Avenue Project will be helpful in illustrating the differences between these choices.

During the 1960s, a coffee house for teenagers was operated in the building that was later to be used by the Project. Dependent upon volunteers, the program was able to operate on Friday evenings for several years. Offering folk music, table games, Ping-Pong, billiards, rooms for discussion, and refreshments, the program was quite popular. But the volunteers dwindled. The responsibility soon fell upon fewer shoulders, and the program was terminated. A few years after this, in June, 1974, some of the same participants of the former coffee house assisted in the development of the Park Avenue Project, a new coffee-house ministry intended to relate with young adults. This time it was decided to proceed with a paid staff, which enabled the offering of a comprehensive program operating during six nights instead of one.

Accountability was built into the new staff's job description, which meant that responsibility for planning, implementing, and evaluating was no longer left to the inclination of a volunteer staff. The difference which a paid staff made for the Project was in terms of continuity of leadership, accountability, constant program development, and a comprehensive offering to the community in the way of activities and services.

Some forms of young adult ministry can function very well without a paid staff. In the case of a young adult discussion group, for example, the members might opt for periodic discussions which they facilitate or which are facilitated by resource people they find. For many other situations, however, the tasks of young adult ministry leadership will necessitate massive amounts of time, special training or capabilities, and a commitment which is strong enough to motivate leaders to confront many issues and problems. Those who are organizing a ministry will have to weigh the advantages and disadvantages of a voluntary or paid staff for their own organizational needs.

In order to prepare fully for a decision concerning leadership, it is helpful if people first attempt to determine the needs to which their leaders will be expected to respond. Secondly, a group needs to compose carefully, in detail, a formal description that will model the leadership expectations of the intended ministry. Taking it one more step, the group should then make a decision between a voluntary or paid staff arrangement. Many questions will be asked at this juncture, such as: "Whom do we know who can bring 'effective' leadership to this ministry?" "What kind of strengths are needed in order to fulfill the expectations?" "Would we be expecting too much to ask a volunteer to assume such tasks?" "Is the formal description realistic and humane even for a paid staff member?" Specific qualities which are sought in voluntary or paid staff persons will vary according to the expectations set forth. Emphasis in choosing a person might be placed upon a particular evangelical style, special training or skills, the degree of openness and tolerance, or upon any number of other points of value. Every beginning young adult ministry must finally decide about the issue of leadership on the basis of their own analysis of young adult needs, as well as a consideration of the potential human and financial resources available as a response. In some church settings, it is conceivable that a present staff member's job description might be redefined in light of a congregational decision to move in a more concentrated effort in the direction of young adult ministry.

## Operational Code

Basic to the development of an organizational structure for young adult ministry is a choice of an operational code with which the people who are organizing the ministry will feel comfortable. This area of discussion is focused upon the issue of "approach," a term which suggests atmosphere, evangelistic style, and programmatic agenda. In order to show a degree of difference in terms of operational code, I will offer two hypothetical cases, one involving a consciously evangelical approach to ministry and the other presenting a more secular design.

Jeff was a stranger to the Catholic church he was now entering, but he had heard about the open discussion and prayer group for young adults and he was determined to see what it was all about. After descending a long series of steps, he came to a doorway which gave him a view of the Dungeon, a large basement room with fresh coats of bright colors on the walls, beautiful banners with religious symbols, and very comfortable-looking furniture. A man in casual attire came over and greeted him, saying, "Peace, friend," and then, "I'm Father John. What's your name?" Jeff responded and then was quickly introduced to four or five people out of the thirty persons who were present. When it came time for the discussion period, Jeff was invited by a few of the members to sit with them. The theme this evening was "suffering," and it was introduced with a short lecture on the suffering of our Lord Jesus. Throughout the discussion, Jeff felt really comfortable about sharing his ideas, and the prayer time at the end was also quite open to his involvement. In fact, the whole evening had been a positive experience for him, especially because of the possibility for participation. He realized from his first impressions that there was some interest in combining religion with life in the discussion, but he definitely did not feel offended, scared, or victimized. Religion was included, and he felt good that the nature of the group was based upon that premise.

Cindy was looking through the paper one day and was impressed with an article about a coffee house for young adults which was open every Saturday night. On the one hand, she was eager to attend on the next weekend because of the popular bluegrass band that was playing. On the other hand, she was somewhat suspicious of the kind of place it was, since the article also mentioned that the program was located in the parlor of a Presbyterian church. Weighing her interest in the music against what she could envision as a "religious come-on," Cindy decided to go and to be ready to exit gracefully if the situation became unbearable. Following the signs after entering the church door, she arrived at the parlor and was greeted by a few of the young adult participants. She noticed that no mention was made of God or Jesus in the conversation. In fact, after talking with her acquaintances into the night, Cindy realized that the goal of the coffee house appeared to be focused sincerely upon meeting people and sharing through a developing friendship rather than presenting any religious message. Cindy began to settle down and enjoy herself, especially when she noted that the only religious message during the whole evening was a short line in the announcements saying that the program was made possible through the generous support of the members of the Presbyterian church. Cindy felt that she had now found a new place to frequent where she was accepted, and she actually looked forward to attending other events and sharing again with her new friends.

These two examples give some indication of the differences of operational code which can exist in young adult ministries. One is more verbally evangelical, more prominently arrayed with symbols of the church, and more centered upon a conscious blending of religion and life, but both examples have a warm and accepting atmosphere. Other situations might be even more evangelical in style, or more secular. It is up to each developing young adult ministry to decide in advance about a suitable operational code (atmosphere, tone, agenda, approach), and then unapologetically to put it into operation.

## Goals and Objectives

Early in the life of a newly organized young adult ministry, the governing board must spend a concentrated period of time on the subject of goals and objectives. While the broad and rather philosophical statement of purpose is a necessary element for defining the nature of the intended ministry, it is not specific enough for the channeling of energies in the many directions the ministry might take. The board needs to decide upon goals and objectives in order to effect a more practical dimension and in order to establish a method of evaluating performance in specific areas.

Goals and objectives are formulated within the confines of the boundaries set by the statement of purpose. Goals are general, directional, and conceptual statements which serve to define a number of ends toward which the ministry is expected to be moving. They give a clear description of where the energies of the organization need to be placed. Taken together, the total number of goals of any young adult ministry might be regarded as a delineated form of the statement of purpose, or as several purposive statements within the limits of a larger theme. In distinction from goals, objectives are very specific, achievable, and timebound, and represent the way movement toward any goal is measured. Objectives are written in order to give a definite and detailed plan for advancing in the direction of the goals. When objectives are accomplished, then the goals can be considered to have been well served and the accountability of intentions to have been demonstrated. Now that a brief description has been given, a modeling of goals and objectives will be presented.

At a board meeting of a particular young adult ministry, let's say that the members have had a goal-setting session for two hours and have formulated the following goals and objectives:

*Goal 1*—To brighten the atmosphere of the facility where the young adult ministry is located, keeping the costs as low as possible.
*Objectives*—We will assess the amount of paint needed to do all of

the rooms, choose colors in a democratic fashion, attempt to get some or all of the paint donated, plan to use volunteers, and schedule the job to be done on two Saturdays in the month of March (the seventh and the fourteenth), from 10 A.M. until 4 P.M.

*Goal 2*—To upgrade the present programming.
*Objectives*—We will draw up a survey to gather information about desired programs from participants; the survey will be formulated by the four persons appointed tonight, and then presented for approval at our next meeting; we will plan to use the survey instrument during regular programming hours in the month of February; tabulation will be done and recommendations made by the Program Committee; more specific objectives will be set when we have heard the presentation.

*Goal 3*—To raise money from new sources.
*Objectives*—The Finance Committee will draw up a special proposal for presentation to the six denominational offices in the area; formulation is to be completed by February 16; presentation at the next board meeting is set for February 24; the time for additions, corrections, and copying is two weeks, which means that a mailing to all six denominational bodies can be expected to go out by March 10.

The examples used in this section are concerned with property, program and funding, showing the breadth of focus which goals and objectives can have. In summary, formulated goals and objectives have real value because they give constant direction to a statement of purpose and provide a form of measurable accountability in the preparation and performance of ministry.

## Support Base

Certainly one of the most significant factors which affects the development and continuity of a young adult ministry is the support base, consisting of people, property, money, and another factor called the grace of God. From the very beginnings of a newly established ministry, it is obvious that without a specific place to use, people who are involved as committed advocates or participants, and some knowledge of immediate and potential sources of funds, the chances of organizing any kind of continued and effective ministry are minimal. Recognizing the critical need of a support base, the unexpected way in which property is sometimes shared, people are discovered, and money is suddenly available are often more than interesting; the experience is at times humbling because it becomes prominently apparent that God is caring for the process and making growth possible. Drawing from the experience of the Park Avenue Project, I would like to share some examples of the support base for this coffee-house ministry.

The Project began its operation on the first floor of a huge house donated by Immanuel Baptist Church. While the Project was expected to raise money for utilities, insurance, and maintenance of the building, the church offered the facility rent free, with the option to have the hired director to live on the upper two floors or to find housing elsewhere. Provision of the place has been an absolutely fundamental support to the ministry.

The most substantial external financial support base for the Project has been through the American Baptist Churches of the Monroe Association. Its early and continuous contributions, as well as other donations from Southeast Ecumenical Ministries, National Ministries of the American Baptist Churches in the U.S.A., area foundations, local churches, and individuals, have been a strong undergirding.

Human resources have also been important in the growth of the Park Avenue Project. Musicians and other performers have donated their time and talents; professional and knowledgeable resource persons have offered to lead various group meetings; merchants in the area have supported special Project events; and the women of local churches have supplied prepared foods for dinners and fund raisers. Then there are the participants of the Project who have done a number of weekly tasks (music bookings, cleaning, greeting people, etc.), worked on a number of big fund-raising events, and assisted in the presentation of the Project's story at meetings with churches and foundations. All of this has been done in a spirit of eager willingness. Others have given leadership to the Project by serving on the Advisory Council, the Finance Committee, the Project Board, the Friends of the Project, or other special committees. The presence of many people who have maintained a commitment during the total span of the Project's years is indicative of lasting interest and strong support. Last, but certainly not least in importance, are the contributions made by students from Colgate-Rochester Divinity School/Bexley Hall/Crozer Theological Seminary who have been placed at the Park Avenue Project for a Field Education experience. These persons have added enormously to the depth and breadth of the ministry.

In conclusion, a support base consists of many kinds of resources, the most essential of which are property, people, and money. A support base is important because it provides for a varied human involvement which will unquestionably result in a large number of people for whom the ministry has meaning. A wide support base for any young adult ministry will be deeply appreciated by those who are responsible for the elaboration of an organizational structure and the development of an ongoing program.

## The Covenant

A final point in the discussion of organizational structure is the reminder that many people are covenanting to provide the actual ministry. It is not merely the staff, the members of the governing board, or the supporting churches who are making a covenant and a commitment to the ministry; it is everyone concerned, including the elderly woman who lives next door to the facility and gives two dollars each year, the people of many faiths and perhaps of no faith who support the ministry because of its value to the community, and the many participants who open up their lives and share in the response of ministry. The point here is that no one person or group can really take credit for the increase and growth of a young adult ministry, since the total effect is always a result of many factors, not the least of which is the grace of God. Having an appreciative respect for the many forms of covenant is a healthy way of viewing any young adult ministry.

Those who are involved in the leadership or the programmatic aspect of the ministry must be willing to work together, covenanting to operate within the confines of a particular statement of purpose, observing a chosen operational code, establishing and implementing goals and objectives, and nurturing the possibilities for ministry. When that nucleus of covenanted people are all endeavoring to promote the ministry, even in the eventuality of small disagreements and differences of opinion, then the organizational structure has a good foundation for the promise and practice of ministry.

## Conclusion

Any young adult ministry which expects to develop a base for continuity and a potential for the extension of ministry must surely develop some degree of organizational structure. While one young adult group might feel adequately organized without the use of a common meeting place or the need of specially trained, professional leadership, another group may feel that these elements are absolutely essential. The sections in this chapter are meant to be treated as guidelines for the development of an organizational structure, and not as the requirements set forth in a rule book. They contain observations and examples which are intended to illustrate the actual diversity of organizational structure among young adult ministries and to give some indication of possible choices and directions.

The value of an organizational structure is obvious. It enables a group to function within a framework of order, direction, efficiency, and responsible management. It provides a scaffold upon which all participants can stand and work toward the same purpose. It is important to note that this work never really stops since the development of an organizational structure is a process which continues even in minute forms after the basic structure is established. Goals and objectives will change, leadership might be expanded, and one hopes the support base will be extended. In other words, the scaffolding is moved around a bit from time to time, with improvements, additions, and changes being made upon the structure. Because this activity is clearly a continuing process, and because each young adult situation consists of a different set of factors, every developing organizational structure for young adult ministry will be quite unique.

# 4
# Guidelines for Programming

Just as an organizational structure is necessary for the provision of order, unified purpose, and planned direction, programming is a process which is essential for the attraction of young adult participants, the formulation of an agenda in line with the statement of purpose, and the fulfillment of specific objectives. Programming is vital in the building of a young adult ministry, especially as it represents an attempt to extend the ministry into the community in a way which is relevant. When programming *is* pertinent and meaningful to a young adult population, it will provide the incentive for belonging to the group, sharing, and establishing a commitment. It will be the single most important reason for people responding to the ministry.

Skillful programming is an art, and it needs to be practiced in order to be learned well. The best of planned programming often seems to follow the instruction of the changing seasons, which offers a sense of difference, newness, and excitement as the temperatures and weather conditions change during the year. A program that is fitting to the temperament and mood of young adults during one month may not be the kind of activity desired by the same group a few months later. Needs, interests, emotions, and situations will all change and will demand adjustments and refinements in the program. The material in this chapter is intended to help people acquire basic programming techniques for working with young adults. While it does not offer actual programs which can be lifted in a prepackaged form and utilized, it does offer a number of ideas about how to approach the whole task and process of programming. When these guidelines are thoroughly understood and applied, they will assist in the enabling of effective program planning within the framework of young adult ministry.

## Target Population

The most basic point about programming is that it needs to be relevant and meaningful to the people for whom it is intended. Because this is the case, it is necessary for each beginning young adult ministry first to assess its target population. For example, if a group is characterized as single by choice, well-educated, primarily white, and apartment dwellers, this profile might automatically suggest a few ideas for possible programs, perhaps on the themes of "Alternative Life-styles" or "The Rights and Responsibilities of Being a Tenant." On the other hand, if a group is characterized as married, well-educated, primarily black, Christian, and homeowners, this profile might afford the opportunity for discussing such topics as "The Meaning of a Christian Marriage" and "The Problems Faced by the Black Middle Class," or it may invite the opportunity of creating a neighborhood action group among young adults in the area. In spite of the fact, however, that the characteristics of groups can help to determine some of the general possibilities for programming, the actual programs which are developed need to have the input and the assent of the young adult population. Characteristics can provide a framework for beginning to think about programming, but the participants themselves must be included to obtain specific ideas for discussion themes, events, and unique projects. Only as young adults are involved in program planning will relevance of programming genuinely occur. Thus, from the clear knowledge of each target population, initial ideas for potential programs are contemplated, but then further refined and augmented when young adults begin to shape their own possibilities.

Besides young adult populations with familiar kinds of characteristics as listed above, there are many other, more specialized groups which might be considered as a focus for ministry. For instance, there might be a church which expressly wants to relate with a group of retarded young adults, choosing to design programs in conjunction with the people. Another church might want to schedule a meaningful program with persons in halfway houses in the neighborhood, or with people in mental health facilities who have community privileges. An ecumenical group might decide that people who are recently out of prison need a special kind of support, and attempt to build a Christian young-adults-with-others kind of program. There are really several such groups of people with special problems, concerns, and situations. It would indeed be wonderful if these groups were given definite consideration and attention in an outreach emphasis of the Christian church, since they consist of those people who are so easily labeled as different, strange, and exiled. Because it is common practice to place many of these persons in separated housing throughout American society, even the Christian church tends to forget at times that they exist.

In summary, it is important to determine the young adult population which will be the focus of ministry. It might be a group within the church, a group in the community, or some combination of these. With the characteristics of the target population in mind, a young adult ministry can be developed with several possibilities for programming. However, these ideas will be more completely and finally shaped as a result of collaboration with young adult participants.

## Program Planning Process

Program planning is a process which requires constant attention and should be done by groups whose memberships are substantially representative of young adults. As a result of this kind of participation, young adults will gain a sense of ownership, pride, and commitment with respect to the program. Using the experience of the Park Avenue Project as an example, a discussion of what is involved in the program planning process will now be presented.

The first point with reference to the Park Avenue Project is the fact that *all* of the programming is planned by young adults who are participants in this coffee-house ministry. A group called the Advisory Council, consisting of eight persons who are appointed largely on the basis of representation of different interests and functions, meets monthly with the director and other staff members for the major purpose of program planning and evaluation. There is a great deal of trust of this planning process on the part of Immanuel Baptist Church and other sponsoring organizations, so much so that the only real expectation from the Advisory Council is that it report its program plans and evaluations to the Project Board. This reporting has essentially been a formality, which is evidence that the trust of the Project in the Advisory Council has been real.

When the Advisory Council thinks that programming has become stale, someone usually suggests the idea of "brainstorming." This is sometimes a timed activity, perhaps five or even ten minutes, and sometimes more open-ended. During the time provided, members suggest ideas for new programs or titles for special events in a very short-phrased and free-association manner. With one idea sparking another, people fire out their thoughts in such a rapid succession that a tape recorder is at times more useful than anyone attempting to function as secretary. The resulting list is often quite long and filled with possibilities. With the list before them, the members of the Advisory Council might discuss the ideas then, or hold off all discussion until the next meeting, giving people time to think more about some of the offered thoughts.

Another method of gaining new ideas for programming is through the use of a survey. With a special committee appointed from the Advisory Council, people work on the formulation of a short survey instrument which is designed to gather ideas about interests, produce information about potential programs, and also discover ways in which people wish to volunteer at the Project. This approach is especially valuable because the base from which the information is collected is much wider than the Advisory Council itself. However, survey instruments sometimes give so much new data for programming possibilities that priorities have to be set. With an attempt to judge what programs would most fulfill the Project's statement of purpose and also involve new people as participants, choices are finally determined and implemented.

Still another method of program planning is by the use of committees. These are generally organized by the director in consultation with the Advisory Council, and they are always organized for the planning of a specific event, such as the Project's "Welcome Summer" Arts Festival. With representatives from the Advisory Council, the Project at large, and the general community, the committee meets for a designated number of months in order to deliberate and decide upon all details related to the festival. While legal questions and any major changes of dimension or direction of the festival would be referred to other groups, the committee as appointed tends to make most decisions on its own. It is charged with this responsibility and with the expectation that a report of the plans be shared.

These are a few ideas which others can utilize in a program planning process. Whether the ministry is located in a church building or a community facility, the functional methods of brainstorming, surveying, and working by committees can be practiced. The groups which are given the responsibility for program planning should consist of a good representation of young adults. They will consider a variety of factors: themes, the need for special resource leaders, timing of programs, the cost factor, publicity, and methods by which the programs will be evaluated. They will also take into consideration a number of ideas which are suggested by individual participants to the staff or leadership, ideas which are often unique and good, and sometimes will even include the offer of personal involvement and responsibility. There will be much discussion of these items, sometimes debate, and the program planning group may be required to vote upon specific suggestions, though it should be possible for most matters to be decided by consensus agreement. If the program planning process is utilized, it will bring about new life continuously and allow for the presence of meaning and relevance within the young adult experience.

## Available Resources

There are many kinds of resources which can be utilized for programming with young adults. The first suggestion for a planning group would be to look imaginatively at the following options: available money, persons, property, unique linkages with Christian groups, and special opportunities in each community. First, with regard to money, it is important to know in advance how much can be budgeted for programming, so that limits will be known as various programs are conceived. Though it is difficult to determine an actual budget figure for programming in the first year of a young adult ministry because of lack of experience, much more clarity will be possible in subsequent years on the basis of a greater awareness of what is needed. Actually, a significant amount of programming can be accomplished without the use of much money, working with a shoestring or even zero budget.

There are also many persons who might be considered as resources. First are the young adults who are a part of each ministry. For example, are there people with special performance talents? Is there a person who can lead a class or workshop on the subject of beginning drawing, camera techniques, macramé, or literature appreciation? Does someone in the group have special abilities in drawing up survey instruments for program planning? Secondly, many other persons, young and old, who might be known through the supporting church or through other churches need to be considered. Someone might have an interesting slide show (there really are some) that would be of interest to the young adult group, or another person might want to be responsible for providing refreshments at a special event. Then there is a third area where human resources can be sought, and that is in the community at large. When the Park Avenue Project was once planning a human sexuality workshop, it was decided that psychosexual problems would be a desirable topic. Someone contacted a very distinguished doctor from the University of Rochester, who was not only willing but also eager to come, saying that in several years of practice he had never been invited by a community group to share his expertise. Thus, from these various sources—the young adult group, local churches, and the general community—many human resources can be found.

Property that is available to a young adult ministry can also be an important resource. For example, is there a 16 mm movie projector that can be used? If so, there are a variety of film libraries which can be contacted, offering hundreds of discussion-oriented or entertainment-type films. Many of these libraries will charge fees for the use of their products, and some films will be available free. The Rundel Library in Rochester, for example, offers a huge selection of choice films on loan to people who reside in the area. Other illustrations of property might be a slide projector, a filmstrip projector, a chalkboard, a coffee urn, or a toboggan. There are many kinds of property which, if available to a young adult ministry, will give a greater span of options to the program.

Opportunities for the development of special linkages with different Christian groups can also be a potential resource. For example, a singles group from a local Methodist Church might plan a special program and extend an invitation to single persons in other Christian churches. A primarily white young adult group which is interested in sharing in a more integrated experience may choose to invite a black young adult group to become involved with them in some way. There are literally dozens of linkages that can be made, spanning various durations of time and offering new experiences to participants. Unfortunately, it is too often the case that few groups even inquire about these possibilities.

Another area where resources might be discovered is the community. There will, of course, be differences in available options from one community to another; and the greater number of resources will most likely be found in the larger metropolitan areas. Programming can be planned in conjunction with the services and offerings of libraries, museums, planetariums, theaters, skating rinks, and college or university public events. Permits can be secured from appropriate city, county, or state offices for the use of shelters in parks. Outings and picnics, sledding, cross-country skiing, and horseback riding are some of the events which might be scheduled. Restaurants are often willing to consider a brunch at group rates. This is especially popular as an activity, since people find it interesting to investigate and experience different menus and decors from one month to the next, and because a brunch provides a relaxed, sociable setting for interchange. The actual resources included in programming will depend upon the community where the young adult ministry is situated, and upon a careful examination of the possibilities.

In summary, money, people, property, linkages with Christian groups, and opportunities in the local community represent some of the potential resources to examine and to nurture in the development of programming with young adults. Of these, money is probably the least important factor. At the Park Avenue Project, for example, only a small amount of money is allocated toward programming each year. Nearly everything is donated: performances by musicians, magicians, and dancers; leadership and facilitation of groups; voluntary care of the building and grounds; and the like. Since there has been no precedent for the payment of people for these functions, giving is respected as a part of the code.

## Group Work: Participatory Planning

Participatory planning is a way of involving the members of a group in the determination of specific program directions. It can work only if group members are willing and able to take the responsibility of self-management. Two interest groups which have utilized participatory planning at the Park Avenue Project are the Human Relations Workshop and the Cosmic Dimension. The former was organized to discuss concerns and questions about personal and relational human issues and to provide a supportive community where persons could relax and be themselves. The

Cosmic Dimension was established to provide a unique opportunity for persons to explore religious questions and issues through an open and honest exchange of ideas and to work toward the development of a genuinely personal theology. Both of these groups have been open in the sense that anyone has been free to come and go at any time. Their programs have been scheduled on a trimester pattern, with a different series starting in September, January, and May. The process of participatory planning, utilized in the dynamics of both groups, is explained below.

Since the Park Avenue Project prints a monthly calendar which is available to the community, it is easy to publicize planning sessions as well as actual programs and events. During the months designated for planning, at least two entire weekly sessions are reserved for this function. People who have read the calendar and have decided to share in this process attend; and although all planning nights are apt to have fewer participants than theme nights, there is still a core group of about eight people who become involved in the planning of each series. First, there is a rather long brainstorming session, inviting people to share ideas for possible discussion topics; these will later be refined and titled in ways which will be attractive to new people. A second process involves the question of leadership, which is a choice among the utilization of some of the people in the group, resource people in the community, or some mixture from these sources. While the group has a staff person who serves as facilitator, maintains order, and takes care of group process, leaders are desired who will have previously studied the scheduled topic and will take responsibility for at least introducing the discussion. Sometimes the participants will decide to schedule "open" sessions between two or among several thematic topics; in this case, no leadership is needed, since the group creates its own discussion out of the thoughts and feelings of those present. After all leadership questions have been determined, a third process of participatory planning is begun—the ordering of topics in relation to a natural progression of interest and a fixed set of dates. When this is accomplished, a flier is designed, the schedule is printed, and the plans are advertised.

Participatory planning for group work has been an important process in the life of the Park Avenue Project. Those who have shared in the process have cultivated a strong sense of group ownership and have committed themselves for the definite number of weeks of a particular series. This kind of planning process can easily be used in the development of group work in other young adult ministries.

## Special Programs

In one sense, the designation of "special programs" can refer to the usual type of program for which a young adult ministry is noted. For example, there are ministries organized around particular needs which many people share, such as a single parents' group or a prayer group. In another sense, "special programs" can refer to those which are unusual and distinctive in comparison with the normal offerings of a given young adult ministry. In other words, if a church-based group was normally organized for the purpose of Bible study and discussion, a special program might be a temporary involvement in an action project, such as the visitation of inmates at a local prison. These kinds of programs are special because they are exciting additions to the ordinary.

Young adult groups which by their very nature are special will need to cultivate that focus and identity so that they can be known to others. A group for separated and divorced persons, for example, will have an appeal to a very specific population, and it will be important for the group to reach out far and wide to anyone who is experiencing the same situation. While members of specialized groups will certainly also plan programs which are unusual and distinctive for themselves, they will be most noted for their focused and exclusive appeal to people in the community, and this degree of specialty is what will be appreciated most about them.

The Park Avenue Project is a ministry which offers both of the types of special programs noted above. On the one hand, the coffee house is especially known and appreciated for its music program on weekends (traditional and contemporary folk, bluegrass, country, blues, classical, and jazz). Performances are scheduled every Friday and Saturday night, and people come from long distances to hear their favorite singers and instrumentalists. However, there are also other kinds of special programs which are planned more seasonally around the needs of people. For example, there is the annual Community Thanksgiving Meal which is sponsored through donations from Park Avenue merchants. This meal is for people who do not have family in the area, do not have the money to afford a special meal, or for those who desire to share Thanksgiving with a larger-than-nuclear family. Average attendance has been at least fifty persons each year. Retreats also respond to special needs, usually in terms of people wanting to get out of the city or desiring to have a close, intimate group experience. Those who decide to attend Project retreats completely plan their program all the way from discussion themes to a schedule for cooking and cleanup. A Seder is a special annual event as well, and this is led by one of the several Jewish men who attend the Project. Done in a traditional but informal way, the Seder is a unique experience for sharing and learning among faiths. All of the examples mentioned are annual events, since repetition is regarded as a way of building a meaningful tradition of special programming.

The provision of "special programs," whether this be through a sharply focused group identity or through the design of activities and events in response to special needs, is a way by which a young adult ministry can focus its attention with relevance and meaning. The programs are special *because* they serve the particular needs of a group of young adults.

## Implementation/Evaluation

With reference to program implementation, it will, of course, be necessary to know who will have this responsibility at the time of program planning. After all, it would be fruitless to dream up absolutely beautiful programs and then fail to have any planned way of bringing them into being. If a young adult ministry has a professional clergyperson on the staff, then he or she might be a likely choice for at least supervising the implementation of some programs, and perhaps actually performing the task of implementation for others. Specially trained leaders might be acquired for programs which need a technical, professional, or scholastic expertise. In the case of groups such as the Human Relations Workshop, the leadership and facilitation roles will be fixed at the time of participatory planning.

Besides the question of "who," it will also be important to define the other familiar questions of what, when, where, why, and how. What will be the exact theme Mr. Miller will be asked to lead? When will the Drama Workshop be scheduled (months, days, times)? Where will the next retreat be held? Why have we decided to offer an educational program about the mentally retarded? How can we guarantee a substantial number of participants for next month's special series? When answers to these kinds of questions are known, then clarity about program implementation will prevail for everyone.

Evaluation is a responsibility which needs to be designated in advance, too. It involves the task of judging how well a program was conceptualized, facilitated, led, and received. There are really two kinds of evaluation procedures which most people use. An explanation of these methods follows.

The first is a formal method, which evaluates programs in terms of previously stated objectives. In this case, the program planning process involves the careful composition of objectives which are written in purposefully exact and achievable terms. For example, one objective might be: To have people write a letter to God (2 P.M.–2:30 P.M., March 16), to distribute these letters randomly to others within the group (2:30 P.M.–2:45 P.M.), to have each person read to the rest of the group the letter which he or she chose, and then have the group share perceptions (2:45 P.M.–4 P.M.), and, finally, to offer a time when people can state what they learned about themselves and others (4 P.M.–5 P.M.). The evaluation would take into consideration all of the stated aims of the program—task, time, conditions, learning value— and would determine whether the previously stated objectives were achieved.

The second method of evaluation is more personal in nature and far less stringently related to a precisely stated objective. It is based more upon a judgment of feelings and a quality of experience. Again using the Human Relations Workshop as an example, the practice of the group is to take responsibility for its own evaluation. At the end of a series, people gather into a special evaluation session and ask one another the following questions: What did you think of the series? What sessions did you especially like? Why? How was the leadership during the series? In what ways have you learned from others? Where has there been meaning for you? These kinds of questions are informal, experientially based, and open to a wide range of responses. They represent a quite different form of evaluation compared with the more formal method.

In summary, implementation is an important concern in programming, and each young adult group needs to clarify the who, what, when, where, why, and how for each program. It will also be necessary to know who will be charged with the responsibility of evaluating various programs, and by what method this will be done. The results of evaluations will be extremely useful in the design of newly stated objectives and in the fashioning of more meaningful programs.

## Publicity

With all of the thought and preparation that goes into the creation of a unique and meaningful program, it is important then to consider ways by which others will be attracted to what has been planned. The publicity requirements will not be the same for all young adult ministries since some programs will not be intended to be as open or as publicly promoted as others. In each case, however, publicity channels will have to be chosen in relation to the level of assessed publicity needs. A student Christian group on a university campus, for example, may wish to publicize its upcoming series on ecological ethics, and choose to announce its plans to the student body through the campus newspaper and radio station. A Christian singles' group may desire to advertise its regular meeting time to others, selecting a method of communication involving pulpit announcements on a particular date. A third young adult ministry may wish to publicize a musical program intended for the general community and choose newspapers and local radio stations as channels. In each of these cases, there is a program in need of a definite degree of advertising, an audience chosen to contact, and a method determined for this purpose.

One of the points to consider in the development of a young adult program is the question of whether to have a special logo which will serve as a familiar identifying symbol for the ministry. This is an individual choice, and it depends somewhat upon how widely recognized people want the ministry to become. In the case of young adult ministries which will be widely publicized in order to gain a special identity in the community, the design and constant use of a logo would certainly be of value.

There are several ways which can be used to publicize a young adult program. Within the context of the Christian community, there are church bulletins, pulpit announcements, associational newsletters, denominational and ecumenical circulars, and the communications of a number of specialized ministries. Beyond the limits of church organizations, there are many other kinds of publicity channels available. Newspapers will often have a community events calendar that is free to the public. Radio stations will accept public service announcements from community groups. In both of these cases, it is important to inquire about the form in which the publicity must be sent and about advance deadlines. Newspapers might also be interested in writing a "special interest" story concerning a young adult program. For really unique events, such as the "Welcome Summer" Arts Festival at the Park Avenue Project, television stations should be contacted for advance publicity. Contacts with all of the above sources will need to be initiated and nurtured by the leaders or designated persons in each young adult ministry.

A number of publicity channels have been utilized by the Park Avenue Project. For instance, a logo was developed from the very beginning. This has been helpful in establishing an identity within the community, as the logo has been used on the outside sign of the Project, a specially prepared brochure, the stationery, and most of the program calendars. Probably the most popular publicity channel for the Project has been the calendar of events which lists everything that is happening during each month. This is picked up by participants, sent to newspapers and radio stations, posted in public places, and mailed to a list of subscribers. With all of the methods which have been used at the Project, surveys have clearly shown that most people learn about the programs by word of mouth. Since this is the case, announcements often include the direct suggestion that people tell others about what they have experienced.

A final thought concerning publicity is the reminder that some people have definite experience in this area, and many times they are willing to share this in order to assist a young adult program. Unless leaders or participants are renaissance persons in the sense that they are masterful at a number of jobs, including publicity, there will be several young adult ministries which will have to look for people with special ability and experience in drawing, design, photography, preparation of camera-ready work for printing, writing of news releases, and other basic communication skills.

## Ownership

A middle-aged man once volunteered at the Park Avenue Project by helping out on weekends. He would arrive before opening time, combine all of the ingredients for our unique spiced tea, start the coffee and water urns, straighten up the tables and chairs, set out all of the refreshments, put signs up about who was performing, and then sit at the door for three hours, greeting people and accepting their donations. He did this every Friday and Saturday evening for at least two years. The reason he volunteered was because he wanted to give of himself and feel useful; what he found in return was a deep respect from others and a wealth of meaning in his life. When a newcomer would take a first sip of the spiced tea and comment by saying, "Hey, this is great stuff!", you could always see a proud smile on the face of the man by the door. In fact, he would often be willing to inform new people about the exact ingredients of the recipe. He had a definite feeling of ownership of the program.

Another, a younger man, had been attending the Project regularly on specific nights each week. He would come in and get some coffee, sit down, and generally not talk with anyone. When people attempted to initiate conversation, his usual response was given with very short, sometimes antagonistic utterances. Because of his quietness and aloneness, his concern for the Project was often questioned by others. Since he was not a "team" player, his interest in and identification with the total program of the Project was not considered to be very great. It was at one of the picnics in a nearby park that the opinions of many were changed. During a brief, relaxed conversation with three or four people under one of the shelters, he said, "I guess this is our last picnic for the summer," and then, "We sure have had some good times." The use of the words "our" and "we" was very comforting to hear, since it meant that his identification with the program was much more closely bonded than people had thought. Though he was usually quiet and often removed from the conversations of others, his regular attendance at specific functions had produced a sense of belonging and ownership. But it was not until he was willing to share his feelings through public statements that this sense had become known.

A woman in her mid-twenties attended the Project for several years. In that time, she volunteered to clean, sit at the door, count and roll money, stuff envelopes, help out at fund raisers, and serve as a member of the "Welcome Summer" Arts Festival Committee. She was available for literally anything that was needed to be done. One time when we were sitting together in the Community Living Room, she said, "Larry, the Project means more to me than you'll ever know. The people are important to me. My volunteering here is important. The Project is a big part of my life." Her deep involvement had already clearly demonstrated the message conveyed by her words, but the words were especially important to her as a verbal statement of the sense of meaning and ownership she had found in the Project.

There is also a man who has made a commitment to be present every Friday night in order to help in the greeting process, a woman who has reached for the vacuum cleaner when the rug has shown its telltale signs, and another man who has mowed the lawn time after time with the use of a push mower.

A sense of ownership has come to many as a result of participation. It is found in the form of a strong identification, a feeling of partnership, a bond, a special meaning, or a deep pride. When ownership has been felt within a young adult group, it is a valuable testimony of the establishment of meaning in the program and helps to extend even further the total support base for the ministry.

## Conclusion

Programming is such an important function within the framework of young adult ministry. It is what attracts people and engages their attention and interest. With opportunities to participate in the process of planning, implementation, and evaluation, programming allows people to acquire a sense of ownership, meaning, and commitment. Because of the unique options in the way of available resources in each young adult population, in local churches, and in surrounding communities, programming is always able to build and expand upon initial ideas and designs, and thereby to offer a constant freshness and relevance. With evidence of the development of a special program emphasis and the practice of effective publicity skills, the program of any young adult ministry will become known and appreciated for what it can offer to participants.

In the final analysis, there are elements which are beyond skills and beyond learning which have a significant effect upon the development of any young adult ministry. One of these is the quality of human experience which results from the interchange and association of various individuals who are brought together in a matrix of ministry. No one knows in advance how these interchanges will help a group's development, but they do. They provide the group with a certain form, potential, and growth. The other element, a matter of faith, is that the grace of God is very much involved in the unfolding of the present activities. While efforts can be made to design carefully programs in ways which will be new, relevant, and exciting to people, the life of a group is constantly presented with circumstances and heretofore hidden opportunities which result in the sudden generation of new programming. No person can really take credit for the newness that comes as a result of these elements.

# 5
# Funding

Along with the pleasurable and joyous moments of watching people participate in meaningful programs, there is another side to young adult ministry which is not particularly rewarding and which many times is disliked by the people who are charged with administering a young adult program. This is funding. Part of the reason it is sometimes viewed as a necessary evil and a chore is that many of the people who will serve on the boards of young adult programs will not have had any experience with the work of funding. Because it is so new to some, and because people would often much rather put their time toward the program and person-oriented ends of the ministry, funding seldom attracts willing volunteers. However, because it is so basic to any young adult ministry which hopes to establish a stable identity in the community, maintain a relevant program, cover the costs of utilities and upkeep of a facility, and grow in leadership in response to needs, funding is an area of responsibility which simply cannot be ignored.

The material in this chapter will be most useful to those organizational structures which need to develop many sources of funding for survival. The small young adult church group which has a dozen members and maintains an annual program budget of $150 will certainly be able to learn from the following suggestions, but the larger organizational structures which project operating budgets of many thousands of dollars and which need to consider every available option with reference to their program will stand to benefit most from the reading. The intent of this chapter is to assist people in the understanding of the funding process, provide potential techniques for discovering new sources, and guide people to the point of seeing that there can be joy—even in the work of funding.

## Finance Committee

One of the conditions which Immanuel Baptist Church established at the start of the Park Avenue Project is related to the concern of funding. The condition states that if the Project's budget ever goes into the red, then the program must end. This short and simple rule has kept the Project actively involved in the process of funding and always aware of its total responsibility for securing a base of support from its own participants and from others in the community. The establishment of a finance committee at the Project seemed like a logical way of ordering the energies of people so that special condition would not have to be enforced.

Each young adult ministry operates with its own unique organizational structure and administrative board and sometimes with special conditions, as in the case of the Park Avenue Project. In order to give a focused and continuous attention to the development of a funding base, it is necessary for an organization to establish a finance committee or to designate a few persons to assume this area of responsibility. Of course, a young adult group composed entirely of church members who meet weekly at a church for discussion will probably have their financial needs met in the total church budget; programming costs will probably be covered out of operating expenses which all members are asked to support. The finance committee in this instance will likely be an every-member-canvass committee or the actual finance committee of the church. However, there are many other young adult ministries which will not be able to depend upon a specific church budget for their financial needs. They will instead have to establish their own finance committee, work hard at the job of discovering and nurturing sources, and be willing to learn the lessons taught by disappointment and success.

A finance committee would meet regularly, perhaps monthly, for assessment, planning, goal-setting, implementation, and/or evaluation of the funding process. One of the first tasks of a new committee would be the determination of financial needs in several areas: maintenance (utilities, insurance, repairs, etc.), staff (professional, lay, clerical), program (stipends, supplies, subscriptions, etc.), office and administrative supplies, and so forth. All of the categories of needs would be listed in a budget which records the sources and amounts of anticipated income and also a listing of expected categories, items, and amounts of expenditure. Sources of income for young adult ministries might include local churches, offices of larger church organizations, foundations, individuals, and fund-raising events. If several of these sources are planned to be developed by one young adult group, then it would be wise for a finance committee to delegate responsibility to various people, since it takes a great deal of individual attention, for example, just to contact and maintain communications with foundations or with regional offices of denominations. The specific amounts which are finally decided as objectives for income and fund raising from different sources need to be realistic and achievable. The key to a successful operation is to attempt to raise all of the money anticipated, and more, and to spend no more than the budgeted expenditures allow, and perhaps even less. But the initial budget must be a fair, clear, and accurate statement of anticipated expenses based upon real needs.

Budgets among young adult ministries will vary widely. Potential sources of income will also vary from setting to setting. Each young adult ministry will have to assess its own local resources in relation to perceived needs, and attempt to develop those resources into a base of support. The finance committee will be an important channel in this funding process.

## Church and Ecumenical Funding

Churches, denominational offices, and ecumenical organizations are natural places for young adult ministries to be looking for a base of support, at least for initial funding. Members of these various Christian bodies are often eager to see new ministries develop and are willing to give consideration to the offering of seed money in the first year or two. Sometimes a new ministry will not be fully understood by a few members of these groups, as in the case of an intentionally secular ministry, but trust and openness are often present in a degree which is sufficient for a vote of support. Recognizing the right of Christian ministries to emphasize different aspects of theology and to employ a variety of approaches to people, the members of these Christian groups often show a tolerance and sometimes a genuine appreciation of these differences.

A young adult group which is located in a church and open primarily to church members will normally look for program support from the church budget. Another young adult group which is comprised of separated and divorced persons, based in a Baptist church and open to participation of persons from other Baptist churches, might look for support from its own church and from a local Baptist association of churches. A coffee-house ministry which intends to serve any young adult in the community, regardless of faith, would probably go to all of the churches in the community, choosing to make initial contacts through the offices of regional church organizations. The sources of income which are approached in each case will primarily depend upon the population being served. If a young adult ministry is totally open, attended by people of many faiths, and unique to that community, then it has every right to inquire about the possibility of funding support from several religious groups. It all depends upon the claims of programming and service a young adult ministry can offer.

There is much work involved in the contact of these sources. Calls have to be made. Materials explaining the ministry need to be prepared. People from the finance committee and from the general program must be willing to meet with mission committees, outreach committees, and others who desire a personal presentation about the young adult program. The staff of a young adult ministry might be invited to preach or to address various church groups. In the event that money is given by churches and larger church organizations, there will be a need for people to go to these groups periodically with a report which provides both an update for those who already know about the ministry and an educational experience for those who do not. Paragraphs might also be written regularly for church newsletters or for the mailings of larger church bodies. Communication needs to be done constantly, and done well.

It is important to discover as quickly as possible the formal process required by denominational and ecumenical groups with respect to funding requests. Some applications will be very long and very demanding of information, and these will necessitate many hours of composition. Other forms will be quite short, but complemented by a thorough and exhausting interview process. Deadlines for the receipt of the material will vary from one organization to the next. Once a young adult group discovers what formal procedures there are, it will be crucial for the group to follow the list of requirements to the letter.

When presentations are made before these organizations, the

members will be looking at a number of elements: the nature and purpose of the program, the potential for financial self-sufficiency, the effectiveness of the staff, the value of the program to the community, the sincerity of the presentation, and the commitment of leaders and participants. All of these elements must be stated or shown in one way or another (slide show, question and answer period, stories from the ministry, etc.), which means that thorough preparation for presentations would be an essential and valuable exercise.

## Program-Initiated Funds

A question which is asked of many young adult ministries by those who hear funding requests is, "What are you doing for yourself?" People want to know how much money is being raised through programming, how many participants are involved in working for the support of the ministry, and whether or not plans have been conceived for the continuous raising of such moneys. This is a reasonable query; it assumes that a vibrant young adult ministry will have the commitment of its participants and leaders even in the area of finances. It is quite unlikely that funding sources will seriously consider giving money to a young adult group if its members' only answer to the above question is "nothing."

Program-initiated funds are essential for at least three reasons: participation, ownership, and group respect. When special fund-raising events are programmed by a young adult group, they allow for meaningful participation by group members. When people have worked on several of these events and begin to feel that their participation has been a significant contribution to the maintenance of ministry, a sense of ownership develops. When the people of a young adult ministry can point to specific events and amounts of moneys raised by participants, funding sources will surely have a respect for those efforts. Thus, the development of program-initiated funds has the potential for yielding many positive and valuable effects for a young adult group.

The Park Avenue Project can provide several examples of program-initiated funding, since it was early in the life of the Project that this pattern of funding was developed. The Advisory Council, rather than the Finance Committee, has largely taken the responsibility for designing and planning these fund-raising programs and events and also for implementing them with the help of many other

Project participants. Attempting to organize special events which would be good enough and popular enough to schedule annually, the Advisory Council conceived of three major festivals which were planned for different times of the year. The first of these is the Annual Pre-Groundhog Day Benefit Festival Weekend. Scheduled for the weekend before Groundhog Day, the festival in its first year offered three evenings of folk music and old-time movies, hamburgers (called groundhog burgers) and other refreshments, and an opportunity to experience an enjoyable evening in the midst of a winter season. The event was very popular and has been repeated in many subsequent years. Project participants have helped by cooking, serving food, taking money, serving as emcee, and greeting people. Over $700 was raised in the first year.

The second event in the calendar year is the Project's largest programming fund raiser. Scheduled in early June and called the "Welcome Summer" Arts Festival, this two-day event has included craft exhibits, live music (folk, bluegrass, jazz, and classical), concession stands, sidewalk sales by merchants, and a parade. To illustrate some of the growth, the first year's festival had thirty-five craft exhibitors, was located on part of one city block, and realized a net income of $610. Net income for the second year was $2,400. In the third year, the festival had sixty craft exhibitors, live music plus another performing arts area, a special dixieland music performance at night, a large parade, sidewalk sales, and merchant involvement that expanded the festival over a ten-block area, a free minibus to take people up and down the avenue, and free maps of the area listing all scheduled events. This time the net income was $3,500. People participated by cooking or serving at the concession stand, selling balloons, setting up, cleaning up, and in many other ways. About forty volunteers have helped out in any given year.

The third event is another music festival held on weekend evenings sometime late in October. Designed much like the Pre-Groundhog Day Festival, the event has offered a mixture of folk, jazz, and blues, and also special refreshments. Although the nature of the festival has never changed very much, the weekend has been given different names: "Autumn Equinox Minus Four," "Autumn Awakening" (with one dinner performance), and "Shades of Blue." People have looked forward to this time of year because they identify the season with this Project event; many like to participate as volunteers and many more enjoy just listening.

What is similar in these three Park Avenue Project events is that they are all fund raisers designed to capture the popular, shared interests of many people. Scheduled at different times during the year, each of these events has become an important tradition to hundreds of participants, and in the case of the summer festival, thousands. They have offered unique ways for raising program-initiated income and also for improving upon program-initiated income levels in subsequent years.

There are likely to be a number of young adult ministries which will never have to think of organizing fund-raising events as large as the ones described above. For example, a one-day car wash might raise all of the money needed to cover the annual program expenses of a young adult group composed of members from one local church. And a dinner dance might raise much of the money needed by another young adult group which is ecumenically comprised. However, the important point here is that, regardless of the size of the group or the breadth of its constituency, program-initiated funds can help to fill the voids of budgets needed for young adult ministry. They can provide a means for participation, a sense of ownership, and a way of gaining the respect of others. Program-initiated funds are an important aspect in the development and growth of a young adult ministry, especially as the generated activities give opportunities for people to join hands and work together.

## Slide/Tape Show

When making presentations before churches, larger church organizations, foundations, and other groups, statements about the program and work of a young adult ministry should be clear, concise, and descriptive. Since people who have the job of listening to dozens of funding requests constantly must be reading proposals and meeting with dozens of groups on a sometimes tight schedule, it behooves anyone who is making a request to design a presentation in as short and effective a form as possible. A slide/tape show of a young adult program is an excellent resource for developing this form of presentation, since it is visual, audible, short, and to the point.

Many people have worked on the preparation of the Park Avenue Project's slide/tape show. First, three or four persons offered to take the pictures. Armed with cameras and very good amateur photography skills, they were able to capture a variety of happenings and moods: folk music, the community living room, group meetings, the finance committee, special fund-raising programs/events, the staff, volunteers at work, movie nights, game nights, holiday activities, and so forth. The slides are representative of what happens at the Project, and those who see them almost have a feeling that they have visited the coffee house. Second, a committee was given the task of writing a script which would tell the story of the Project and then of choosing slides to be used in conjunction with the script. Last, a tape was made which included readings of the script as well as background folk music, and this was synchronized with the showing of the slides. The final product was sixteen minutes in length, showed every aspect of the Project's life, and answered most questions that would have been asked with a strictly verbal presentation. The slide/tape show was made possible because of the energetic work of about a dozen Project volunteers. It has been a source of much pride as people have taken it and shared it with many groups.

After the slide/tape show was ready, as many showings as possible were scheduled—to the mission committees of churches, the American Baptist Churches of the Monroe Association, Southeast Ecumenical Ministries, and several foundations. At these meetings, there would be a short introduction of the Park Avenue Project and of the slide/tape show, then a running of the slides, and finally a question and answer period. The director, members of the finance committee, and participants from the program would all be present to field questions and to talk with people individually once the meeting was over. Given the concise nature of the slide/tape show, the total presentation has often been effectively accomplished in thirty minutes or less.

This method of presentation has been extremely effective. It has enabled the Project to fit into the sometimes tight schedules of business and finance meetings. It has given a visually clear and broad picture of the Project's activities, an audible statement of where the Project is and where it hopes to be, and a definite feeling for the work of this ministry. Because of the effectiveness of the presentation, most groups feel that further inquiry or site visits are really unnecessary, and many have been willing to consider seriously funding the Project. The slide/tape show has been the single most important resource of the finance committee, because of its portability, its condensed format, and its effectiveness. While the presentation has been primarily used in connection with an appeal for funding support, it has also been shown to groups who just want to learn about the program of the Project. In this case, it has an educational value which is vital to the development of a greater awareness of the ministry and a potentially stronger human support base. Thus, the slide/tape show has been helpful in promoting a wider understanding of the Project as well as providing an excellent resource for securing funding.

## Foundations

Foundations are another source of possible funds, at least in the initial stages of organizational development. Managed by its own directors, a foundation has the purpose of maintaining or aiding programs and activities which are educational, charitable, social, or religious in nature. In order to learn about the purpose and practice of the many foundations which may be available to a young adult ministry as financial resources, several hours have to be given to a research process. In preparation for this research period, it would be advisable for a young adult group to determine first with absolute clarity what its own purpose is and what specific levels of funding will be required from foundation sources. Only when this task is accomplished will the research process make any sense.

Most all of the research concerning foundations can be done in a public library. For example, the Foundation Center prepares and publishes *The Foundation Directory,* a standard reference work which has been published in several editions since it first appeared in 1960.[1] Foundations are listed by state, in alphabetical order, with information as to address, purpose and activities, financial data, and names of officers. Additional books of a comprehensive nature will also be available as reference materials, and some of these are included in a special listing in chapter 8.

More specific information about foundations can be obtained through looking at the information returns filed annually by private foundations with the Internal Revenue Service. Form 990-AR provides the address of the foundation, the names and addresses of foundation managers, total assets, and a list of grants. Form 990-PF also includes much of this information, but it is more concentrated in providing financial data, giving complete lists of grants made during the year, as well as a record of financial transactions. Available on film which is filed on aperture cards, these forms can be examined by use of a microfiche reader. Although hours of this kind of research can do an injustice to one's eyes, the information does help in making a judgment as to how the purpose and program of a particular young adult group might compare with those who received funding, and also whether the initial thoughts about a request figure are on or off the mark. Details about where reference collections of this kind are located are also included in chapter 8. One suggestion is that initial research efforts might be focused upon local foundations, since they will be much more convenient for establishing communication, and since they will already have the local interest at heart. People should also be aware of any foundations which might be set up in large churches, since these may have an inherent interest in supporting a community-wide Christian ministry.

Funding requests to foundations are usually presented in the form of a proposal, a document which contains detailed information concerning the ministry. The style and format used at the Park Avenue Project include a two-page general introduction followed by an index of exhibits. These exhibits are presented in a definite order, and they include information about the Project's uniqueness, population profile, program and objectives, fund-raising objectives, impact on community life, case studies, organizational structure, special needs, prospects for funding, and a financial statement (complete budget); exhibits are then followed by endorsements and other entries. This format works well because it allows a foundation the choice of reading and referring to selected exhibits. Placed in a binder along with a covering letter addressed to the contact person and stating the amount of money requested, the proposal is easily sent to many different foundations with only minor changes in the covering letter. Once written, the proposal is a very effective instrument in the communication of information about a young adult program, but the writing takes hours of effort and really needs to be done with care.

Foundations all have different deadlines for the receipt of proposals and definite procedures for reviewing requests. After learning the name of the contact person, these matters can be clarified as well as any other expectations which are unique to the foundation. In the covering letter, it is important to convey a willingness to meet with members of the board and answer any questions through a formal presentation. Foundation personnel may also be invited to visit the young adult program when it is in full operation, as this will provide a firsthand experience and knowledge of the ministry. If a grant is extended from a foundation, it may be given under the condition that a specific report be sent about how the money has been used. In any case, whenever money is dispensed, all accompanying instructions will need to be followed and prompt thank-you's will be very much in order.

There are a few strict requirements and limitations in the giving of a foundation grant. For example, the officers will want to know whether the potential grant recipient has an Internal Revenue 501 (C) 3 tax-exempt status. Since practicing religious groups can easily qualify for this status, Christian churches and the ministries which they organize and support can certainly be viewed as potential grant recipients. However, there are also young adult ministries which are more separated and independent from the church. A secular ministry, for example, might prefer to establish a low-profile identification with church organizations and religious expression. In order to be considered as a grant recipient in this case, the ministry might have to establish its own identity as a not-for-profit incorporated group and then attempt to qualify for a tax-exempt status. Another limitation which many foundations may clearly establish is that no grants can be made toward the operating budgets of organizations. In other words, unless part of a program can be designed which represents a new and unique venture, or an entire young adult ministry can be shown to be absolutely unequaled in terms of conception and promise, then it is doubtful that some foundations will make a grant. Many foundations will also desire to know whether funding requests might just as easily be honored by grants from the government, or from other sources. Each young adult ministry which is hoping to receive money from foundations must discover what requirements and limitations there are, decide whether the whole process is worth the time and effort, and then abide by that decision. If the decision is affirmative, people will have to be ready to do the work that is necessary to secure a foundation grant, prepared for the experience of disappointment, and content with the likelihood of having to cherish a few very happy and successful moments.

## Other Sources: Government and Private

Because of the separation of church and state in America, government sources of funding would be among the least likely to be available to young adult ministries. Programs which are strictly geared to a particular denomination or expression of faith would have inherent and automatic reasons for denial of funding requests. In order to qualify for government funding, a young adult program would typically have to be a recognized entity that is nonsectarian, nonevangelical, and not for profit. While a young adult program might truly be considered as a ministry by the staff and sponsors, government agencies will not give it much consideration unless the purpose is defined and shaped in terms of a community-oriented and secular focus. Programs which are able to qualify for government funds will have to approach those agencies which best represent their own interests. One young adult group might apply to ACTION for a mini-grant, if it can identify with the purpose of helping to mobilize part-time, uncompensated volunteers to work on human, social, and environmental needs, particularly those related to poverty. Another young adult program might apply to the National Endowment for the Arts or to a State Council on the Arts, if it has, for example, a primary interest in the performing arts or a specific interest in developing a community-based cultural event. Those who qualify for this kind of funding should bear in mind that there are forms, deadlines, and reports which will be a part of the experience of requesting and receiving government money.

There are a number of private organizations which might be willing to give some support to a young adult program. Depending upon how unique a service is provided to the community and how broadly that service extends, the Community Chest is a possible source of funding. If an organization passes its qualifying criteria and becomes a member organization, the Chest can furnish a good deal of financial security for a number of years. Of course, there will be a reporting and a monitoring of funds required of each member organization. Other private sources which might consider making a donation toward the support of a young adult ministry are the fraternal groups, such as Kiwanis, Lions, Elks, and Masons, or the many service organizations such as the Jaycees. Finance committees will have to be thorough in assessing the potential of local organizations for helping with the funding base.

Finally, individuals can be an important source of funds. For example, there might be a very wealthy woman who is a member of the local church where an emphasis is placed upon a young adult ministry; she might be willing to contribute substantially to this work, and possibly more than once. Then, too, there might be a small, little-known private foundation whose principal officer is a member of the Lutheran church where a young adult group meets weekly to talk about the meaning of faith. If this person, or others who have a special connection with private resources, can somehow gain an understanding of the value of such a group, then a new funding source may suddenly be discovered. Many times, out of a belief in the worth of a ministry, members of the staff and program participants will convey this message, even without consciously thinking about it. On the basis of these shared feelings, sponsors and patrons are often developed.

Individual participants and advocates who are on the boards of various organizations can be quite valuable to young adult groups, especially if they are willing to speak positively from their experience with a young adult program. Then, too, there are always key people who are well known in the business community who will have access to the offices of top-level organizational people. As advocates of a ministry, some may be willing to invite their friends to a special tea or to a game of golf and utilize the time to convey a message of personal commitment concerning a specific young adult program. It has to be realized that certain individuals are in a natural position to express the meaning of a ministry to persons who might normally be difficult to contact.

## Friends of the Project

Most of the income at the Park Avenue Project in the first few years was realized from church organizations, foundations, and special fund raising. When individuals happened to send periodic contributions to the Project, they did so on a purely voluntary basis without the bidding of an established pledging system. Individual donors included program participants who would give to the general operating expenses or to a specific need, such as the partial payment of an event's advertising costs, and also nonparticipants whose awareness of the program was sufficient to interest them in maintaining a supportive role. Since contributions were beginning to come from these sources, the finance committee reasoned that a number of people might be willing to give to the Project if there were an organized way for making this kind of commitment. Thus, a Friends of the Project group was started.

With volunteers managing the work of the new organization, several approaches in the way of appeals for new funds were planned. The first approach was focused upon the people who normally attended Project activities. A poster was made in order to bring attention to the new organization, and forms were made available which explained the group's purpose and invited people to register as a "Friend." Quarterly mailings were sent to people who registered, informing them of current progress at the Project and presenting them with general financial appeals. A significant amount of money was raised through this initial effort.

The first major undertaking to expand the number of Friends beyond the program participant base was through the design of a mass appeal. Concentrating upon a definite geographical area which bordered the Project on all sides, letters of general appeal and program materials were sent to the names of residents found in a current listing. The purpose was twofold: to educate the community about the program of the Project and to begin to build a group of individual sponsors from the area. From the three thousand letters which were sent, only a small fraction of the recipients returned a contribution; yet the new income was sufficient to pay for the mailing, enabling many people at least to learn about the Project, and brought in several hundreds of dollars. The appeal represented a huge amount of work on the part of volunteers and at least a fair return of income; the total effect of the activity was so positive that one could only say that it was well worth the energy. Besides the value of people having worked together on this mass appeal, the Project now had an expanded list of patrons.

Later in the development of the Project, and within the limitations of one calendar year, the American Baptist Churches of the Monroe Association offered to contribute up to five thousand dollars to the Project on a matching basis, thinking that this would be a. way of increasing the number of "Friends" even more. With the provision that for every one dollar raised from individuals through new pledges three dollars would be given from the association, the finance committee and other participants began dreaming up special ways to encourage giving. One of the most unique was a five-mile HIKE FOR ECOLOGY which found a host of hikers walking along city streets, trash bags in hand, picking up debris and litter. Hikers were responsible for securing one or more sponsors who agreed to pay a specific amount for each mile hiked. Donations which came in through this hike were treated on a matching basis, and the "Friends" group was again expanded.

Friends can be established in almost any organization. For the Project, this group has been an important vehicle for receiving donations from individuals. It has also afforded to many persons the opportunity of feeling good about being a sponsor or patron. Most important, it has been valuable in building a greater sense of ownership on the part of program participants and advocates.

## The Self-Supporting Base

A frequent question posed to young adult groups who appeal to organizations for funds is: "What are the chances of your program becoming self-supporting?" It is asked by church organizations, foundations, and many other groups, and the way the question is answered can often weigh heavily in the determination of ultimate funding. It is asked because funding organizations do not want to encourage the development of a ministry which becomes totally dependent upon others for survival needs and because they want to acquire an accurate reading of how a young adult ministry is succeeding with a program/participant support base.

In anticipation of this concern, each young adult ministry needs to consider seriously whether it has the potential for becoming self-supporting. Can the costs, for example, of building maintenance, staff salaries, and program be wholly sustained through special fund-raising events? Can the costs be partly sustained in this way, and is there a possibility of growth in the percentage of income which is raised in this manner? In the case of a young adult group within a local church, is there an activity that can help toward the provision of a self-supporting base for the group's program costs? Each young adult ministry has to decide on its own what the answer to the posed question is. If a group can honestly state that a self-supporting status is possible in the future, this will be well received by funding organizations. If a group with a multi-thousand dollar budget, on the other hand, cannot make such a statement, but vows to expand continuously the self-supporting base as much as possible, this too will be appreciated. It will be important, most of all, to respond in an honest fashion. Let the funding groups know of previous self-supportive programs and also of any immediate plans and goals made for these kinds of activities. Let them know exactly what the likelihood is for becoming self-supporting.

Having a self-supporting base is valuable, as participants will be involved in the support of the ministry. People will offer ideas about fund-raising events and volunteer to help in their implementation. An appreciation of what is involved in the building of an organization will be acquired as people enter into the work of raising a budget.

Participants will feel that they are pulling their own weight and will develop a healthy kind of pride concerning their efforts. They will gain a sense of ownership of the program and of the total organizational structure for ministry. The self-supporting base will also be a strength for young adult groups as they go before various organizations with funding requests. It will be evidence that a young adult group is not asking for a handout. It will illustrate that a group has integrity, pride, and commitment, and that everything possible is being done by program participants in the support of the ministry.

Again, the potential for becoming self-supporting will differ from one group to another. However, regardless of these differences, every group can share in the goal of striving to become more and more self-supporting. Every young adult ministry has some potential for helping to provide its own financial support base.

## Conclusion

Funding is an important consideration in the development of a young adult ministry. While it may be thought to be a form of drudgery when people first look at the fund-raising needs of their young adult group, it soon becomes an activity which is appreciated for its share of joys. For instance, there is a tremendous feeling of accomplishment and rejoicing when the members of a finance committee receive word that their specially prepared proposal has resulted in a grant from a foundation or from a church organization. There is much fun associated with the task of creatively designing fund-raising programs which will be popular because of their uniqueness. There is a sense of excitement and challenge when program participants roll up their sleeves and begin to assume at least some of the responsibility for the maintenance of a ministry. Funding is anything but drudgery if people are involved in the process and the work is shared by many.

If a young adult ministry must raise a large annual budget, the finance committee will have much work to coordinate. Members will be writing proposals and letters for sending to church organizations, foundations, government agencies, and/or private groups. They will be nurturing the development of program-initiated funds and involving others in this process. They will be making presentations to various groups by means of a slide/tape show, or in some other manner, with the purpose of telling the story of the young adult ministry. They will be working on strengthening the giving of individuals, aiming special appeals to participants and potential advocates. Members of the finance committee will have a full agenda, especially in the case of large and complex organizational structures.

Regardless of the size of a young adult ministry, there will have to be an assessment made concerning funding needs, and members of a group will have to be ready to assume a number of essential tasks. In the midst of the organized funding effort, there will be some disappointments, and they are normal. But there will also be joys.

# 6
# Models of Ministry: Ways of Relating from the Church

In order to give some idea of the variety of potential forms of ministry which are possible with young adults, several models will be described. The first six models will be illustrated in a story format, using created situations which have given moods, characters, motifs, and settings. The reason for this approach is so that a genuine feeling for what happens in young adult ministry can be conveyed through the material. Following these six models, there is a final section on innovative ministries. Because of the number of examples to be presented in this section, there is a shift back to a more descriptive format.

All of the following examples of young adult ministry are based upon known models. However, the stories which depict the models are creations invented from a blending of many experiences. Names used in all stories are fictional. The section on the Park Avenue Project is also a composite of many experiences and does not refer to any particular persons who have frequented the coffee house.

Besides being helpful to people who hope to work with young adults, this chapter will also be of value to those who are already laboring in this form of ministry, since it gives a broad perspective of young adult work and contains ideas which might be able to be applied in a number of community settings. Those who now work with young adults will especially be able to relate to the stories on the basis of somewhat similar experiences.

## Young Adult Church Group

The Reverend Dan Fisher walked out of his Brooklyn apartment and headed across the long and familiar stretch of four blocks. He waved at Lennie at the gas station, but otherwise he did not pay attention to anyone on the street. There was too much to think about on this Friday night, and he was determined to use the walk reflectively. By the time he arrived at the door of his small United Church of Christ building, he was fairly sure of what he would say to the young adult group at seven-thirty. Since there was still another half hour left before the meeting, he thought that he would busy himself in the church office while continuing to weigh his thoughts.

After about ten minutes, Steve and Janet Jacobs walked into the church and promptly peeked into the office to say hello. Dan responded with, "Hi, how are you doing?" The two remained silent for a short time and then Janet said: "Not so good, Dan. You see, Steve and I have been thinking about this group, and we're not sure that our interest can be sustained with the way things are going. There is something that really seems to be lacking in the program." Although Janet had been somewhat nervous about confronting Dan in this way, she seemed to be relieved when he stated that he was having similar thoughts and was even planning to take some time for a discussion on the theme of group purpose that very night. Satisfied that there was some possibility for their concerns to be heard, the Jacobs thanked Dan for his time, excused themselves, and walked toward the church parlor to wait for the other members of the group.

By 7:30, twelve members had arrived and Peter Wagner, the elected leader for the year, called the meeting to order. Announcing that Dan Fisher was scheduled to lead a discussion at 7:45 on the subject of "The Urban Christian," he asked if there was any quick business that needed to be covered. Janet Jacobs immediately stood up and, looking around at the other members in the circle, said, "Steve and I would like the group to address what we think is an important question—and that is the group's purpose."

Peter instantly considered how long this kind of discussion might take and looked over at Dan for a cue. Since Dan was hoping to encourage this kind of exchange on the basis of his own concerns, and because he felt that the question of the group's purpose was certainly germane to any discussion about the urban Christian, he responded that it would be very fitting to use the time to deliberate on this issue. He suggested to Peter and the other group members that the discussion might begin immediately and that a formal consideration of the scheduled theme be put aside for the time being.

Janet began by saying that the group experience over the last three months had been valuable to Steve and herself. They were especially happy that the group consisted of both black and white participants, since this factor offered a special dimension not found in other church groups to which they had belonged. Then, too, they thought that the group was special because there were single persons, including the minister, mixed in with couples. Steve, who had been nodding in agreement with these statements, then suddenly added: "What Janet has just been saying is a necessary background for the hearing of our concern; in the simplest words, this group has been very meaningful to us, and we want you to definitely know that." Some of the group members indicated an appreciation for hearing Steve's statement; then there was a pause.

Janet soon broke the silence by offering the following summary of their dilemma: "We are not happy to think that this group is merely concerned with weekly discussions and periodic cultural trips. Not that these haven't been enjoyable, mind you, but they don't completely satisfy our expectations for the group. The discussions challenge our minds and educate us on certain topics; yet there has been no opportunity to act on the basis of our Christian faith. In other words, the talking doesn't satisfy our need for feeling involved and committed as Christians. And we have the same problem with the cultural trips. It is thrilling to see a show like *The Wiz* on Broadway and to take in some of the finest cultural offerings in the world here in the Big Apple; yet this sometimes really seems like such a luxury when there is so much need all around us."

At this point Dan requested that Janet attempt to phrase her and Steve's suggestions in a manner which could help the group think about a possible revision of the statement of purpose. Taking time to choose her words carefully, Janet responded: "Steve and I propose that the group continue to have social times, discussions, and cultural dimensions included as activities. However, we would propose that the group also attempt, at least from time to time, to find ways by which we can reach out and begin to be in touch with the community."

When some of the people asked her to give examples of what she meant, Janet said that perhaps the members could all sign up as FISH volunteers and help people who are really in need of human services. She also referred to the possibility of the group sponsoring a local teenaged basketball team and then taking a real interest in the lives of the players. After a moment, Janet's thoughts began to spark additional suggestions from other people in the group. In fact, the young adults became so excited about the new sense of purpose that they appointed a special committee to begin to consider some of the different options mentioned for involvement.

Dan Fisher felt good about the evening's discussion. While he never did have the opportunity of presenting a message about "The Urban Christian," he was thoroughly convinced that the topic had been covered. He was quite pleased as he walked home that night, pleased with the serious consideration given to the question of purpose and with the group's desire to establish its own direction.

## Young Adult Community Group Meeting in a Church

About one year ago, a young woman called the office of a local American Baptist church in Cleveland and said that she would appreciate having an opportunity of scheduling a meeting with the minister. She gave her name as Georgia Brown and asked if the church secretary could make an appointment for the following Wednesday. When the day arrived, she did some final thinking about what she was going to say and walked into the church at the appropriate time, hopeful that she would find a minister who would be receptive to her concerns.

Following the church secretary into the pastor's study, Georgia was not able to see the minister until she passed through the office doorway. She was somewhat surprised when she saw a woman behind the desk. "Hello, I-I'm Georgia Brown," she said, trying to appear calm.

"I'm Helene Bowers," said the minister, smiling and extending her hand. "Very happy to meet you. Please sit down and make yourself comfortable."

Georgia sat and composed herself. Then she began to tell of her situation as a single parent, stating that no one really understood what problems she and many other people were having to face. She explained that while there were a large number of single parents in the community, there was no group experience available for the sharing of problems and possible solutions. There was no support network that could assure her that people are not alone and that there are others who are able to understand and to care about her situation.

The pastor really heard Georgia's concern, and she offered the use of the church building as a meeting place for a single parents' group, as long as Georgia would consider assuming the organizing and leadership responsibilities. Georgia thought about this suggestion for a few minutes and then did agree to it. She was in a very grateful mood when she left the church.

That was one year ago, and in the time since that day in Rev. Helene Bowers' office Georgia Brown has worked very hard to organize a group experience for herself and others. With the help of the principal of the elementary school which her son attends, she was able to find ways of contacting eighty-seven other single parents. Calling a first meeting and expressing her primary concern that a regular group experience be available to single parents, she was happy to find that nearly all of the young adults who attended shared the same concern. They were delighted to think that a person would carry her own concern to such an extent that it would finally involve them. Some also expressed appreciation over the fact that the pastor had been so accommodating in providing a place for meeting.

The group decided to meet on every other Thursday night at the church. They talked about the special responsibilities of single parenthood, how fathers or mothers had to assume both roles. They invited guest speakers to the group who could help to interpret their experience and give them some direction. At times, they scheduled potluck suppers and brought their children so that they could meet other families with the same dynamics. Every so often, Rev. Helene Bowers would sit in and listen to the expressed concerns. She would also ask her new friends if they would like to attend worship and other special events at the church. There were a few evenings during the year when she was invited to speak about the place of values, ethics, and religion in life. There was no doubt that much good had come from the group during the course of this one year, and the members were so happy that they decided to schedule a special event in honor of their anniversary, inviting all of the current membership list of sixty parents.

Since the anniversary date fell on a Friday, the group thought that it would be fun to have a special banquet in the church basement and to pay to have the event catered by some of the people in the congregation. The parents arrived at 6:30 P.M., wearing their finest clothing. They sat at tables that were beautifully decorated and enjoyed one of the most sumptuous roast beef dinners they had ever eaten. The night was special. What they appreciated most was the realization that they were together as an important support group.

After dessert, Georgia Brown tried to call the group to order so that she could say a few words. With some people wanting to maintain a party spirit, it was difficult at first to get everyone's attention. But silence finally came, and Georgia was able to offer her thoughts: "I'm sure that you all agree that it's been a wonderful evening. The food was fantastic, the service was excellent, and the setting was beautiful. However, I want to get away from the food and the experience of tonight for a moment, and take you back to a year ago, to a day when I was fortunate enough to meet a person by the name of Rev. Helene Bowers. You all know her, and you can see from her presence here tonight that she cares for this group. Well, I just want to say 'thank you, Helene,' because the growth of our group received its roots and its nurturing from your willingness to help us along. We appreciate your support and your presence in this community."

At the end of this statement, the members stood and applauded. Helene then stood and addressed the group: "It means a great deal to me to be here tonight. You have all worked hard to keep this group going. Some of you I have come to know as new members of this church and that always makes me happy. I consider all of you as friends, and hope that you think the same of me. Thank you for your kind words."

Later that night, when Helene was talking with her husband, she remarked about how important that single parents' group had been in the life of the church. It had brought in new members. It had offered to pay a nominal amount toward the utilities. It had illustrated to the community that the church cares.

## Coffee-House Ministry: Secular Mode

It was the middle of January in Rochester, New York. Gary Dunlap sat huddled in his cold and tiny apartment, thinking about how rotten life had become at thirty-one years of age. Just two months earlier he had been living with his wife, Shirley, and their two children, waiting together for the joy of the Christmas holidays. Gary had thought that his relationship with Shirley and the kids was fine, and that their home in Fairport was as happy as any home could be. But he had been wrong. He must have been wrong, because here he sat in a small apartment, away from his family, in the middle of winter. The snow was piled high outside, and the ice on the walks gave the impression that misery was here for at least a season. He was becoming more noticeably worried and depressed about his situation as each day passed by. Desperately wanting to talk with someone who might be able to lift his spirits, he inquired of another tenant about where he might go to find informal counseling. The woman he asked told him of the name of a nearby coffee house, a place called the Park Avenue Project.

Hating the idea of going out into the crisp weather, yet knowing that he had to try to do something for himself, Gary trudged through the snow on the way to the corner of Park Avenue and Culver Road. All along the ten-block hike he wondered about the kind of people he would meet and what he would say and whether he would truly feel welcomed. As he approached the intersection, he saw a house on each corner and wondered for a moment whether he had gotten the right directions. But then he observed a small sign attached to a tree in front of one of the houses and also that this house was more lighted inside than any of the others. While walking up the front steps and into the entryway, he could hear music playing, some kind of folk or country music. A man then opened the door and greeted him.

Gary stood just inside the door and listened to the music for a few minutes and then nervously asked if he would be able to talk with someone about a personal concern. He was not really sure about coming on so directly, but he knew how much he was hurting. The man took him to another room right away and introduced him to the director, a bearded man in his thirties, who was quite open and friendly. They talked for a few minutes and then went to a more quiet area of the house.

In the space of about a half hour, Gary revealed his story. He spoke about how much he loved Shirley and their children, Carlene and Dennis. He seemed to stress that being laid off from work had not helped the home situation, since this had created a potential for friction to develop.

However, because the Project director was having a difficult time understanding why Gary's lack of job security made Shirley want to force him out of the house, he began to probe into the situation.

"Gary, how did you react initially when you were laid off?"

"With anger," he responded, "and with fear."

"Did the lay-off create any changes in your behavior?"

"Yes, I guess so. I was a bit ornery at times, maybe a little hard to get along with."

"Did you begin to drink more during this time?"

With an embarrassed and telling look, and with choked words, he said, "Yes, I guess that's true, but I didn't know what to do with myself. I didn't mean to hurt anyone."

"Are you still drinking, Gary?"

"No, not now. I've stopped that. It's done way too much damage."

At the end of this questioning, the director told Gary that he would be available at any time to talk with him. He spoke about the program of the coffee house and of the many new people he could meet by attending regularly. Gary thanked him earnestly as they walked out of the room.

Left on his own to enjoy the music and what the coffee house had to offer, Gary looked around at the homey atmosphere. There were rugs on the floors, curtains in the windows, and soft, comfortable chairs in the Community Living Room. Walking into the front room where the bluegrass band was playing, he sat down at one of the café tables and immediately liked the atmosphere: candles, tablecloths, paintings on the walls, an appreciative and responsive audience. He was beginning to think that perhaps this place could have the possibility of lifting his spirits in some ways. By the time midnight came, he had had the opportunity of talking with Donna, a member of the Advisory Council, and also Roy, one of the volunteers. Picking up a brochure and a January calendar on his way out, he thanked Donna and Roy and also the director for their help and then said "Goodnight."

The next morning when Gary awoke, one of the first things he did was to study the Park Avenue Project calendar, because he wanted to plan some of his evenings in order to withstand the pain of being alone. He thought that the Make-Your-Own-Pizza Party sounded good for Sunday night and that perhaps on Tuesday he would take in the Human Relations Workshop. Putting the calendar down for a moment, he picked up the brochure and read every word about the Project's philosophy and program. Looking at the back page, he was surprised to find that the director had the abbreviation "Rev." before his name. He was not bothered about this because to his knowledge the Project's intent was not to force religion on anyone. He was mostly intrigued because the Project seemed to be caring and helpful and interested in offering a special kind of accepting atmosphere.

On Sunday night Gary was eager to go back to the Project. When he went inside, he noticed that Donna was there, along with about twelve other young adults whom he had not met. Seeing Gary come in, Donna stood up and greeted him, and then introduced him to the whole group. Since it was time to go into the kitchen and start making the pizzas, everyone got up and found new seats around the large kitchen table. The director had already been there for the past few minutes and with his wife was making final preparations for the pizza toppings. He said "hi" to Gary and to others who had recently arrived, and then he explained the process for making the pizzas. Working in twos, with each couple designing their own toppings from the assortment of ingredients, people would bake their pizzas and then share the results with everyone who was present. Gary really enjoyed this experience, since he was included in the group in a way that seemed natural and nonthreatening. He was beginning to feel an acceptance at the Project.

After a few visits to the Human Relations Workshop on Tuesday nights, Gary decided to attend the group regularly. Led by a female middler student from Colgate Rochester Divinity School/Bexley Hall/Crozer Theological Seminary, the group seemed to provide a genuine opportunity for open and honest dialogue about issues within an atmosphere of trust. Some of the men and women in the group were able to understand Gary's present situation because of having had similar experiences. It was an uplifting feeling for Gary to meet people who were so caring and to be told that there would be a time when he would not be feeling so low. It was good to hear that happiness did not have to be permanently absent from his life and that his self-esteem and confidence could surely be restored.

By March, the snow in Rochester had begun to melt and the temperatures began to rise above freezing. Gary's apartment was more tolerable, and he even took some time to do some minor but cheerful decorating. A job offer finally came from one of the many applications he had made; so he was happy to consider the possibility of a regular income again. His first impulse upon receiving the job offer was to call his wife and tell her, and perhaps be able then to make amends. After all, he still felt that he loved her, and he also wanted to be in touch with his children. Well, Gary did call, and he talked and talked and talked with Shirley, but it was just too late. She did not want to consider resuming the marriage relationship.

Contacting the Project director by telephone, Gary asked if he could talk with him right away. Soon they were sitting at the Project together, and the hurt was spilling forth in tears. The realization that his former relationship was definitely ended was just too shocking for Gary to handle. After a while, he was able to calm down, and he thanked the director for listening. They soon began to talk more positively about how Gary could go on living by affirming life. The director reminded him about his children who were meaningful to him, the people of the Park Avenue Project who helped him get through some rough times, and the presence of God who has provided a special kind of strength.

After that day Gary Dunlap became an even more active participant in the Project, helping out at fund raisers, offering to help lead groups, and greeting newcomers as they entered the coffee house. While the divorce process was a difficult experience, he had friends with whom he could talk. And after a time, he was married to a woman by the name of Jewel Morton. The wedding service was held at the Project and the Project director officiated.

When the couple announced that they were intending to relocate in Los Angeles, Project participants had mixed feelings. They were sorry to lose such a good friend and a willing worker and happy that Gary had regained his purpose and confidence in life. They were convinced that a part of the Park Avenue Project would always remain with him.

## Coffee-House Ministry: Evangelical Mode

Homer Linfield was drunk. Having walked the downtown streets of Boston for two hours and finishing off his supply of liquor on the way, he was now tired and almost completely senseless. In fact, he was in such a bad way that he suddenly thought that he was hearing the voices of angels. After listening for a long while, he realized that the voices were really human and were coming from the doorway just ahead of him. Unable to make out the sign on the door even when he got there, he boldly stumbled through the entryway in order to hear the voices at a closer range. Two young men, when they noticed that he could hardly stand up, went over to help him.

"Hi, I'm Scott Reynolds," said the man who stayed with him. "What's your name?"

Very slowly, he said, "Ho-mmm-er."

"Well, the Lord sure does work small miracles, Homer, because you fell into good hands tonight. How about some coffee?"

Nodding at the question and saying "reg'lar," the coffee was brought to him immediately. Sipping it and savoring the aroma, he began to smile a little.

"Praise the Lord," Scott affirmed while Homer drank his coffee. "Praise the Lord that you're all right."

Scott sat at the table for nearly two hours, nursing Homer to sobriety. Finally, when Homer was able to listen to reason, Scott suggested that he sleep in one of the back rooms for the night. "It's just a couch, but it's comfortable," he said.

"Much obliged," Homer responded, and when he lay down, he was sleeping soundly almost immediately.

When Homer's eyes first met the light of day at seven o'clock, they focused upon a banner on the wall. It had the symbol of a fish on it and a loaf of bread. He tried to think for a few minutes about the night before and could only remember a kind of spiritual music and the help of a man by the name of Scott. Looking around the room, he observed banners and posters with religious sayings on other walls. Not sure of what to make of the whole situation, he stood up and ventured into the next room.

"Homer, I see that you're feeling better," said Scott upon seeing him. "How about some coffee? And we've got some donuts, too."

"Yeah, please, and—thanks," said Homer, as if in pain. "By the way, what kind of a place is this?"

At this invitation, Scott sat down with him and presented the story of Fishers Mission. He explained that the mission was named after the biblical image of Jesus leading his disciples to become fishers of men. The mission staff consisted of born-again Christians whose purpose was to extend the saving message of Christ to as many people as possible. Open twenty-four hours a day, every day of the week, the mission especially wanted to reach young adults, since there seemed to be so many people in their twenties and thirties who were confused and searching. Scott then began to direct his concern to his new acquaintance: "This is essentially a coffee house, Homer, but we're here for more than the enjoyment of a cup of coffee. We're here to bring souls to Christ. We try to offer a spiritual atmosphere of gospel music, reading materials, group discussions, prayer and fellowship, and all for one reason." Pausing for a moment, he then said, "What about you, Homer? Have you known the Lord? Are you aware that with God's help you can overcome any kind of a burden, including a drinking problem? Do you . . ."

Homer sat there and mainly listened. Scott went on for a long, long time. Then Homer said that he needed some time to think it all over. He thanked Scott for the help and told him that he would plan to return to Fishers Mission to see him another time. Soon he was gone through the doorway, back to the familiar street life of downtown Boston.

Later that day at the mission, Scott Reynolds chaired a meeting of most of the staff. Scheduled to last for about one hour, the purpose of the meeting was to bring everyone up to date with respect to each person's experience of the Lord's work. There was first an open time of prayer when everyone was invited to participate, and then Scott offered a closing prayer. Asking what people had experienced in the last couple of days, he waited for someone to begin the sharing.

"I've got a few things to relate," said David Tompkins, a person who worked on a shift which was different from Scott's. He then told about a new child prostitute who was working in the area with her older sister. The girls were only thirteen and nineteen years of age. They had been into the mission two days ago and had shown at that time a genuine interest in hearing about the Lord. After fully explaining about the prostitutes, David then mentioned, with a saddened face, something about a young, twenty-four-year-old, pan-handling drunk who was killed just that afternoon when he walked into the street in front of a car.

"Oh, Lord, please—no!" said Scott. "Do you know his name?"

"I think it was Homer somebody," said David softly.

Scott explained why he was concerned, and then he asked if everyone would please join him in a time of prayer: "O God, our Father, who is loving and merciful, have mercy now upon Homer, for he was a sinner. He drank, Lord, but his body was not satisfied. He was young, but he was aging so quickly. Help us, Lord Jesus, to be able to reach people before tragedy comes. Help us to feed and clothe the stranger and the hurting, and to be with the lonely, just as you said we should. And help us to find a way to speak to the *hearts* and *souls* of the people who come into Fishers Mission, so that we may be your instruments of love and peace. O Lord, we know that you have your reasons for taking Homer at this time. But grant to us some understanding and peace as we think about his presence here just last night. In the name of Jesus the Christ, our Lord and Savior. Amen."

The meeting went on after the prayer, and others told about their experiences with evangelism through the unique coffee-house mission. It was always an interesting meeting. There were the many stories of confusion, hurt, pain, and suffering on the part of young adults who frequented the mission, and of how the mission was able to help, even if only sometimes temporarily.

## Satellite Churches

Lance was seven years old, and he was determined to help his mother make preparations for the church meeting to be held in their home that evening.

"Mom, I want to help make the punch!" he said, excitedly.

In a very obliging manner, Cara Winkler included her son in the work. She liked the thought of Lance taking part in this way, since she felt that the church was important for both of them.

They worked hard at the preparations, doing some housecleaning, setting extra chairs in the living room, and putting out dishes and silverware for coffee and dessert. They were planning to host one of the satellite groups of the Fireside Church, a group which practiced a contemporary folk form of worship and met in various members' homes on a rotating basis each Thursday evening. This particular group chose Thursday as a family worship time because families were then allowed the freedom to enjoy their weekends together, and the satellite group as a whole could plan family-oriented outings and retreats every so often as well.

While Lance was busy for a moment, Cara reflected about how fortunate they were to belong to a religious group that was so meaningful. She knew that there were thousands of people across the United States who could not say this because they belonged to congregations which were too large to meet individual needs or because they were alienated from the Christian church and still searching for a meaningful group. Of all the offerings in San Francisco, she liked the Fireside Church best, mainly because it was so tailored to personal needs. Organized in satellite groups consisting of no more than thirty members each, the church was encouraging a pluralistic approach to Christian worship and living. Besides the folk worship, other groups were formed around classical/traditional styles, dance, drama, and avant-garde techniques. While the membership of these satellite groups primarily consisted of young adults, Cara did not really mind this concentration, since her overriding concern and priority were clearly that meaning be present in her religious practice. Her thoughts were suddenly interrupted when she heard Lance trying to open something with the electric can opener. She quickly went into the kitchen to see what was happening. "Here, Lance, let me get that," she said. "I'll let you pour the juice into the punch bowl after the can is opened. Okay, hon?"

Not very long after the punch had been mixed, the doorbell signaled that the first guests had arrived. It was Billy and June Caldwell and their son, Tim. Billy had wanted to come a little early so that he would be sure to have his banjo in proper tune. Next through the door were the Irwins. Margaret and John were responsible for the order of worship tonight; so they too were anxious to arrive a little ahead of schedule. John had made special plans for involving the children in the service, and Margaret had taken the time to search for meaningful readings drawn from the Bible and from the works of favorite poets. After a while it seemed as though the doorbell was never going to stop ringing. It was getting near to the seven o'clock worship time, and Cara was busy making sure that everyone was comfortable.

Margaret Irwin, seeing that nearly everyone was present who was expected to be, announced over the busy conversation that worship was about to begin. John was able to gather the seven children in a short time and seat them at one end of the living room, on the floor. With a total of twenty-four persons filling the room, Margaret first took time to explain the order of worship for the evening. After she was finished, she invited everyone to start by joining in the singing of one of the group's favorite songs, one that was written by Billy, entitled "Sweet Light of Jesus." Although special songbooks had been prepared by the group for its worship, everyone seemed to know this one by heart. Billy plunked away on the banjo and provided a moving accompaniment to the full sound of singing in the room.

The remainder of the worship included many different parts. Margaret asked people if they would read some of the selections which she had marked. There was a time for open sharing of how people felt that God had been present in their lives during the previous week. John had all of the children sit in a circle and play a game which required them to learn and remember ten different Christian symbols. The adults watched the game in progress and were able to learn from it as well. There was a group meditation on the theme of the suffering servant. The first part of this was meant to be absolutely silent, and then the members were invited to share openly what they thought. Billy Caldwell led the group in four other songs during the service, and the people were very appreciative. Margaret ended the service with a unison recitation of an updated version of the Lord's Prayer. Then everyone stood up—men, women, and children—and gave each other loving and supportive hugs, saying in the process, "Christ is with you!"

Coffee and dessert were always served after the worship; so the atmosphere now became more social. Lance was busy helping to fill the punch glasses, and Cara was waiting on the adults. Cara thought to herself for a moment about the name of their church—the Fireside Church. She was sorry that she and Lance were not able to offer a real fireplace as a setting for worship. However, she knew that the members did not really need a hearth. They felt warm and happy just by being together.

## Campus Ministry

Chester Band is a black campus minister serving a local United Methodist church and a large college campus in Indiana. Half of his job description is focused upon the young adults at the church, where he is an associate minister in a multiple-staff situation. The other half is focused upon the student body at the college, where he also works with a multiple staff, taking responsibility for relating with students in general and Methodists in particular. While the split job description is a difficult burden to expect any person to assume, Chester has been doing well with it for the past two years. He actually prefers the situation because it allows him to work in more than one circle. He also likes it because it provides a good opportunity for the students, giving them a person with whom they can relate both on the campus and in the community. Chester has been able to work well with white students as well as black students, and his popularity as a campus minister rates very high.

One day while Chester was working in his church office, a thirty-four-year-old white member of the congregation, named Priscilla Davenport, stopped in to see him. It seems that she had been thinking about the possibility of having the church host an all-day (Saturday) seminar on the theme of ethics, and she wondered if this would be the sort of program that students might want to attend. Chester indicated that he thought so, and he responded even more affirmatively after Priscilla explained the nature of her proposed seminar. Her suggestion was that many different fields of ethics might be offered as an attraction for specific interests and that everyone would be expected to attend the morning discussions about ethics as a guiding principle. She envisioned the day as an opportunity for church members, college students, and community residents to join together in a very special way. Chester and Priscilla worked hard on the preparations, scheduling planning meetings, checking with the appropriate church boards, working on the details for the seminar, and finally beginning to advertise the day's activities and to register people.

On the Friday before the seminar, all of the registrations were counted. There were twenty-seven students, twenty-one church members, and fifteen other people from the community at large. Of the twenty-seven students, Chester observed that four were members of the Black Caucus; nine belonged to an evangelical Christian group called Living Light; six identified themselves strongly with an activist group; and the rest did not seem to represent any particular persuasion. The schedule for the day was planned to include a brief presentation on the basic building blocks of an ethical system given by Professor Marion Robbins, a member of the religion department at the college. From that point on, people would remain with the interest group they had chosen. The five groups would be formed around the themes of eco-justice ethics, sexual ethics, biomedical ethics, ethics and technology, and life-style ethics. Although many students had registered for sexual ethics and there were many church members signed up for eco-justice, there was still quite a mix of persons in each interest group, and the groups seemed to be roughly the same size. Chester and Priscilla were both looking forward to the next day, for they had great expectations that the unique mix of registrants was going to prove fruitful to everyone.

Sixty of the sixty-three registered participants showed up the next morning, ready to begin the day's activities. Professor Robbins started the seminar off according to plan, and his presentation was well received by nearly everyone. Two people felt that they had to argue with him about the way he had diagrammed the building blocks, but apart from this there was no real dissatisfaction. After a mid-morning coffee break, each scheduled group gathered in their assigned room and began their discussions under the leadership of designated persons. During the meetings of these groups people were able to share from their deeply felt personal perspectives. For example, a young man by the name of John Kasey, who was an adherent of the Living Light, got into a verbal conflict with an eighteen-year-old church member, Susan Brown, over the issue of premarital relations. In another group, a very vocal male activist student was angering a man from the community because he was appearing extremist in the choice of methods he would use to bring about justice in the town where the college was located. In still another session, there were a number of people involved in a debate about whether values necessarily had to be altered because of technology.

At the end of the seminar, when everyone came back together into a large group, Chester allowed for a time of sharing concerning the day's experience. Most participants were in agreement that while there had been differences of opinion stated within the five groups, much growth had occurred. During these meetings, people learned not only the variety of thoughts that others held about ethics but also that an appreciation and respect of many positions were possible while holding onto one's own values. Chester and Priscilla were pleased about the day, especially what came out during the last plenary session.

The long-term effect of this event was much greater than expected. More students became excited about choosing the local United Methodist Church as a church home. The church's young adult group decided that it would like to take responsibility for sponsoring other activities similar to the one proposed by Priscilla. Everyone was more appreciative of Chester's role as a minister, since the seminar enabled people to see the value of his dual involvement and the special skills which he brought to the ministry.

## Innovative Ministries

Shifting from the story format, brief descriptions will be given of several young adult ministries which can be classified as innovative. Some of these ministries are so specialized in nature that they attract attention as being different; the others are called innovative because they seem to be created out of pure imagination. All of the innovative ministries which appear in this section have at one time or another been proposed and designed by Christian groups within the United States. Many of them are currently being employed.

## Apartment House Ministry

Because young adults are just starting out with careers and often have not accumulated enough money for a down payment on the purchase of a house, a large proportion of them must resort to living in apartments once they have left the family homes in which they were raised. Apartment house ministry is primarily geared to working with people in their own surroundings by attempting to meet the residents of a particular building and then create meaningful programs, activities, and services. Depending upon the population with whom a ministry is working, the concentration of the program might be in any one of several areas, including religious discussion, health and welfare issues, referrals to helping agencies, education about the rights and responsibilities of tenants, urban gardening, the formation of a bike and hike club, and so forth. Although tenants might be suspicious at first, most people will eventually respond to a genuine interest in helping them, and an apartment house ministry will have almost limitless possibilities once a level of trust is established.

## Laundromat Ministry

Many young adults have to lug their clothes down to a local laundromat once a week. While there, they spend a majority of their time waiting upon machines and generally feeling bored. A Christian group which decides to purchase a laundromat has a unique base for meeting people, scheduling special programs, and developing a ministry.

## Runaway Ministry

It is not uncommon for a significant number of young people to run away from the safety of their parents when they decide that it is too much trouble to try to live at home in peace. Communication gaps between parents and youth are often wide, and the sense of caring love is not felt to be present. Many teens sacrifice food, clothing, and security just to be able to be free. In desperation, some turn to drugs and to prostitution, and a vicious cycle is started. Runaway ministries attempt to locate and care for people who are stranded, hiding, and at the mercy of whoever will offer temporary housing and security. Although youth are primarily represented in the age span of those who become labeled as runaways, the ministry has been mentioned here because young adults are also involved.

## Marketplace Ministry

Young adults who are unemployed, on drugs, or confused about the direction their lives are taking will often spend time meandering through malls and shops and sitting for long periods in deep concentration. Appearing to most passersby as though they are seeking momentary rest, they are many times sitting in those public places in order to kill time. With nothing to do, no purpose in life, and no future that looks very favorable, many people attempt to blend in with the furniture and to look busy for the lack of anything else to do. Marketplace ministries have befriended people, learned of their situations, provided referral help and direction, and have demonstrated that the Christian church is active beyond the bounds of the church building.

## Bar Ministry

This is a more controversial form of ministry, since many Christian people could never feel right about participating in it. However, the rationale for a bar ministry is clearly sound. Proponents hold that because many young adults drink, and because a surprising number of people become alcoholics at young ages, it makes sense to consider a bar as a potential arena for ministry. Because many lives are lost or are being lost in a bar, the corollary holds true that the potential for helping people is great. Through the purchase and operation of a bar, or through the consent of a bar owner, a person in such a ministry can come to know many people and carry Christian concern and helping skills into the community.

## Ministry to Streetwalkers

Those who have been involved in this very specialized ministry to prostitutes have primarily attempted to serve as a friend. Meeting with young adults in restaurants and bars, ministers have been able to offer genuine friendship, trusted advice, and someone to talk with when life has been especially difficult. Considered and treated as outcasts by large segments of society, men and women prostitutes have at least been able to feel the care of the Christian church through this kind of ministry.

The innovative ministries listed in this section are a representative sampling of what has been happening recently in young adult ministry. As more and more people become involved in working with young adults, additional kinds of ministries will surely develop. Each person or group must attempt to assess the felt needs of a specific young adult population, envision what could be an effective ministry, and begin. The most important consideration in a young adult ministry is not that it can be labeled as innovative but rather that it can be regarded as a genuine form of caring that is able to relate with others in relevant, meaningful, and effective ways.

## The Church in the World—The Tie That Binds

The models of ministry illustrated in this chapter are examples of how Christian people have organized to create a presence with young adults. They show that the Christian church is already in the world in supportive ways and confirm that the church is a motivating force which has the potential for addressing the needs of many different young adult populations. The church is the tie that binds all of these models together, since it has raised people in the Christian faith, provided motivation for ministry, and given important resources in the way of personnel, property, and finances. Adding such examples as military chaplaincy, clinical pastoral counseling, and work in the criminal justice system—all of which also affect young adults in some ways—the work of the Christian church with young adults is spread out in many directions. Sometimes, just as we fail to see the forest because of the trees, we fail to appreciate the magnitude of the Christian ministry because we are looking at only our own local situation.

The important issue which has to be faced by the Christian church with regard to young adult ministry is the matter of priority. Churches have to decide whether they will foster and nurture the development of new young adult ministries, or instead be satisfied with the isolated examples of these ministries which have been able to bud, blossom, and give growth. The problem is that while we do have a forest full of strong and living samples of young adult ministry, the growth is actually sparse. However, if more and more people become concerned about young adults and organize to work with them in unique forms of ministry, the possibilities of providing for growth will be greatly increased.

# 7
# Conclusion

In this brief chapter, I want to direct my attention to "you": you who have thought seriously about young adult ministry, you who have taken the time to read this book, you who sit and wonder even now what to do as a result of this reading.

## The First Step

As a reader of this book, you are one of a group that probably includes people of many different backgrounds, who have a variety of interests in the specific field of young adult ministry. You might be a lay member of a black Baptist church, a white Presbyterian church, an inner-city Catholic church, a rural Methodist church, or some other congregation which has special meaning to you. Then again, you might have been reading about young adult ministry because you have been charged with responsibility in this area by an association of churches, an ecumenical group, or a denominational office. You might be a pastor, a youth worker, a young adult committee chairperson, or a person with no formal connection with the Christian church at the present who just has a desire to see something done with young adults in the local community. I hope this book *will* reach the broad range of persons and backgrounds just described, since this will mean that a greater potential will then exist for increasing the communication about and possibilities for ministry with young adults.

You who have been seriously considering the possibility of working with young adults or organizing local or regional resources so that others can work in this area have probably been feeling the tension between the known needs of the present and the envisioned future. On the basis of reading chapter 1, you may have developed a rationale for ministry with young adults, and a feeling of motivation, readiness, and commitment concerning this area of ministry. However, you might not yet have acted upon your feelings. You may, in fact, still be preparing for young adult ministry because of last minute questions about how to proceed. It is natural to hold back and wonder about all the details and even the rightness of the involvement, whether it be one person or an entire group which is deciding to act upon this kind of commitment. However, without some form of action, all of the reading and preparation is really of little use, and all of the talking and pledging of involvement finally just amounts to empty words. The serious consideration of becoming involved in the work of young adult ministry must at some point culminate in the taking of a first step. If you have sensed a strong theological mandate for your involvement, then surely you must also believe that your actions will be continuously encouraged and undergirded with the strength which God is able to give.

And what shall constitute a first step? Any action which leads you into full involvement in the work of young adult ministry would be considered a first step. You may be someone who has envisioned a coffee-house ministry in your community and now must consider taking this idea to a church board or a meeting of a larger church organization. You may have discovered a particular young adult population with special needs and be questioning your desire to begin communicating and relating; the group might be runaways, singles, single parents, married people, a drug-dependent group, persons experimenting with alternative life-styles, or some other concentration requiring attention and special need. Or, you may have an interest in providing special skills, such as fund raising, to a young adult group. You may want to assist with a special event such as a festival, volunteer for regular activities, lead a certain kind of discussion group, or organize the whole schedule of a young adult church program from planning stages to evaluation. There are really many kinds of first steps which might be taken, and each one is just as important as the other. Whatever does constitute a first step in your case, you should act upon it and allow your sense of commitment with young adults an opportunity to be channeled into a form of practical expression.

In many cases, you will be piloting the possibilities for young adult ministry in your own community. There might not be any local examples of ministry to draw upon as you begin to plan for the building of a special kind of work with young adults. There might not even be any persons who are trained to work with certain needs. As you begin, you will have to bear in mind that many people will be watching and interested in seeing whether your program will be successful. Because new programs often receive this kind of attention, you will be illustrating ways by which other young adult ministries might be able to program with similarly successful methods.

As you contemplate the first step, think in terms of the potential value which might be realized by becoming involved in a young adult program. Think of the people in the current situation whose lives might be helped through the development of a ministry, the raising of program money, or the assistance of volunteers. I remember well, for example, a coffee house for youth developed in the small town of Brookline, New Hampshire, back in the early 1970s. Called the Purple Haze, the program operated out of the American Legion's building and provided a juke box, refreshments, and a place to gather and talk. People in their late teens would come from long distances to be there on weekend nights. The value of the place was that youth were no longer hanging out on the streets and were now connected with a base of friendship and a potential source of trusted advice in the leadership. In the Park Avenue Project, also, young adults have found a place in the community with an atmosphere that is warm, accepting, and nonthreatening, a variety of programs and activities which are planned to be relevant and meaningful, and a human base of friendship, understanding, and support. Sometimes, the value of a first step can best be appreciated only after you realize the effects of intentional involvement.

## The Second Mile

Going the second mile is a familiar directive within the Christian church (Matthew 5:41). It refers to a kind of love and concern for people which does not stop with the least amount of effort which could possibly be extended. The second mile is symbolic of a Christian love and concern which attempts to be fully and completely present with people and supportive in meeting a real need. This kind of symbol is especially appropriate to the development of young adult ministry, because the needs are so vast, and because the Christian church is now called upon to extend itself through unique and sometimes unseasoned models of supportive ministry.

In the first place, going the second mile needs to be stressed in the educational program used to prepare a congregation for possible involvement with young adults, especially at the time of covenanting for the support of a new ministry. Much information is usually shared about the observed needs of a particular population, the possibilities for leadership and programming, the sources of anticipated income, and the way in which a ministry is intended to be organized. However, besides presenting the initial ideas concerning the design of a ministry, the emphasis must be made that the envisioned idea for ministry will have to be given more than ample time to be tried and subsequently judged as to its value. If people in a congregation will want to close down a young adult program because of one isolated and unfavorable incident, or because of the extra cleaning which is required as a result of the extended use of a church building, then it will be obvious that going the second mile was not considered as a posture for congregational involvement from the very beginning. When a church enters into a covenant to bring a particular form of ministry into being and lend support to its continued existence, then it really needs to make the commitment pertaining to that covenant. The ministry must be given every reasonable opportunity to illustrate its potential and value.

Another way in which the second mile directive may be extended is concerned with the matter of tolerance. For example, are there people in your church who simply cannot understand why some young adults prefer to grow beards, wear jeans and informal clothing, or enjoy a certain style of music which is different from their own? Are there people who have difficulty appreciating the fact that others want to express the Christian faith in terms which are unfamiliar rather than traditional? Do some people have trouble thinking about a Christian ministry which reaches out to those who have become alienated and are now perhaps adherents of other religions? In the proposed or developing ministry, is there a pool of differences which might become accentuated and felt and then create bitterness between age groups? This is a very important concern in the building of ministry because these differences, if allowed to be exaggerated, can defeat good and well-intentioned efforts. Since no one wants to see the organization of a young adult ministry become the occasion for a war to begin between generations of Christians, the only sensible option in the planning of such a ministry is that long-standing church members be encouraged to go the second mile with respect to differences and members of a young adult group be forewarned that they, too, may harbor intolerances toward those of earlier generations. If both of these groups can see the value of getting beyond the differences, then the ministry will have a good chance of succeeding. In the matter of tolerance, then, the second mile may also have to be instituted.

A third sense where going the second mile may be necessary is in the invitation of young adults to become active participants in the church. Many churches do not presently have ways by which young adults can become meaningfully involved in congregational life. What the second mile might mean in these cases would include the following:

1. A conscious attempt to involve young adults in all levels of participation: worship, boards of deacons and trustees, Christian education, special committees such as social concerns or missions, etc.

2. A conscious attempt to involve young adults as leaders, as well as members, of various groups. While young adults may appear to older members of a congregation to be too young to be responsibly involved, young adults themselves wonder why twenty-five or thirty years of age is considered too young. At a time when they feel they are reaching their prime in terms of physical stamina, education, and professional training, they need to be given encouragement rather than rejection as leaders of the church.

3. A conscious attempt to formulate a worship experience which would be appreciated by all members and all ages of the church. Separate services might have to be planned, at least in cases where preferences are strongly felt. Or different Sundays might be used to accommodate all of the several preferences over a period of time. Areas of concern would probably be hymns, musical instruments, choral singing, readings, the way a message is delivered, the potential involvement of the laity in the service, etc.

In at least these three ways, then, and perhaps in others, the second mile may have to be undertaken in order to provide a participatory base for young adults in the life of the church.

A fourth situation for the symbol of the second mile is the case of a church which develops a young adult ministry on a community base rather than within its own church building or membership. Especially if the ministry is intended to have a secular focus, the church membership will have to look upon its efforts as a special opportunity to relate with young adults and not as a way of attracting church members. Since the concept of total giving is sometimes difficult for people to understand, even for Christians, a carefully planned educational program must demonstrate the need for the ministry, the value that it can have for participants, and the special form of giving which is called upon in order to provide for the possibilities. In this case, going the second mile would be consonant with the idea of total giving or unconditional mission.

There may be additional ways in which the concept of the second mile would become appropriate in the ministry which you are organizing or helping to develop, and that is something which you and other participants will have to decide. The second mile is a generally needed response in the building of young adult ministry, primarily because of pioneering ministry efforts, sometimes exaggerated thoughts about individual differences, the desire for participatory involvement, and an occasional need for unconditional giving. Thus, the second mile is a gesture of love and concern which is especially appropriate in young adult ministry, and it follows upon the first step. You who have been considering a decision to become involved in working with young adults will have to be ready and willing to exercise both of these gestures.

## A New Dimension

You who are about to become involved in young adult ministry are very important to the Christian church, since as a result of your involvement the church will undoubtedly experience a new dimension. If there are hundreds of you, or thousands, there is good reason to believe that your involvement will create changes and add new life to the church. Although it is difficult to determine in advance what the full significance of scores of new ministries might be for the various Christian denominations, I will nonetheless attempt at this time to offer some personal visions about how the new dimension might be experienced.

The first element of the new dimension created by increased

involvement in young adult ministry would, it is hoped, be a more inclusive church. No longer would churches consist primarily of middle-aged and older people. No longer would a handful of church members rotate from one elected position to another and never allow the opportunity for new participation. No longer would the worship service speak to the needs and interests of some persons more than to others. A more inclusive church would mean that meaningful participation was possible for every member of the church, regardless of differences in age, gender, hair style, skin color, wardrobe, and so forth. A more inclusive church is one in which every person is of value, respected, and appreciated for his or her uniqueness. There are such churches even today, but any expanded work with young adults will surely help to increase the number of churches which decide to become more inclusive.

A second element of the new dimension would be the possibility for the development of intergenerational communication, fellowship, service, and ministry. With young adults attending the church, meeting in the church, or connected with the church by way of a support system, there will be opportunities to begin to erase some of the stereotypes which the younger and older generations often have of each other. There will be times when people will begin to appreciate one another for the persons they are and for the particular gifts which they can offer to the church. When this kind of appreciation is strongly felt, it might be possible to plan specific ways by which young adults can be of service to others in the church, in the same way that older persons initially are of service to young adults in the support of beginning programs. In a church which develops an attraction of people from many different age levels, the congregation can then fully express an intergenerational ministry—a ministry which conveys the message: "I need you, and you need me." This message desperately needs to be heard within the life of the church.

A third proposed element of the new dimension would be a greater understanding of those who are alienated from organized religion. With the church willing to finance or to staff a community-based, secular kind of ministry, there is much insight which can be derived from this experience. Instead of wondering why some young adults are not considering church membership or involvement as a serious option, the church will have firsthand knowledge of the exact sources of alienation. And, instead of complaining about the large number of young adults who no longer attend church or who have become practitioners of religions which are somewhat new and strange, the church can be happy and proud that at least an attempt is being made to remain in touch and to let young adults know that the church is present and caring. With some persons who have become so distant to the church, this is perhaps the only available option as a form of ministry. But it is better than nothing, and it provides the church with at least an open door for beginning to understand and to work with many new persons.

A fourth element of the new dimension would be a domino-effect of model building. As each newly developed young adult ministry illustrates the value of how it is organized and what approach is used in programming, these ideas will be passed on to others. Much of this information will become known by way of denominational magazines, articles in other periodicals, newsletters prepared by young adult ministries, or by simple observation of a particular model of ministry in operation. Models will beget models and refinements will continually be made. As this process of model building occurs, more and more churches will be able to see the ways others have begun to work effectively with young adults, and they will want to consider the same kind of potential in their own situations.

These four elements, then, comprise the new dimension which the Christian church can experience through expanded development in the field of young adult ministry: a more inclusive church, an intergenerational experience, communication with alienated young adults, and model building.

With God's help, we of the Christian church will be able to experience that new dimension, for we know that encouragement and strength will be provided when they are needed. A way will be made known for the development of ministry. New possibilities will arise constantly for programming. Money will sometimes suddenly be made available. All of this does not usually happen without some effort on our part. We at least must be willing to take a first step and then perhaps go a second mile. But let us not forget that God is journeying with us.

# 8
# Resources

This chapter contains a listing of books and of sources of information about films and funding which can be used in the building of a young adult ministry. Subject headings include campus ministry, community study, ministry with young adults, organizational development and management, single life, single parenting, and many others. This compilation is meant to provide a sampling of some of the specific informational and programmatic resources available to young adult ministry. While it is not an exhaustive list, it does give a comprehensive view of the kinds of materials which might be sought and utilized.

Several denominational offices were contacted in the preparation of this chapter, and many responded by sending valuable information. The addresses of these denominational offices have been supplied at the appropriate entries within the listings.

Because prices of materials can fluctuate so quickly, the costs of resources have not been included. Inquiries will have to be made with respect to current prices for books, manuals, film rentals, and newsletter subscriptions, as well as the amounts requested for postage and handling.

## Books and Pamphlets
### Campus Ministry

Gribbon, Robert T., *Congregations, Students and Young Adults.* Washington, D.C.: Commuter Student/Young Adult Ministry Project, The Alban Institute, Inc., 1978. Write: The Alban Institute, Inc., Mount St. Alban, Washington, DC 20016.

Hallman, W. E., ed., *So There's a Community College in Your Town.* Softbound 102-page book on local church ministry with the nearby community college. Write: The United Ministries in Higher Education, Communication Office, 3 West 29th Street, Suite 708, New York, NY 10001.

*Idea Bank.*
Sixty-one page resource book for parish and university ministry, containing over 750 resources and ideas; also *Idea Bank II.* Write: Campus Ministry Communications, Lutheran Council in the U.S.A., Suite 1847, 35 East Wacker Drive, Chicago, IL 60601.

Oates, Wayne E., *Cultural Conflicts of College Students.* A pamphlet issued by National Student Ministries, The Sunday School Board of the Southern Baptist Convention, Nashville, Tenn.

Reklau, Tecla Sund, ed., *Ministry in a Learning Society.* Write: Lutheran Council in the U.S.A., 130 North Wells, Room 2200, Chicago, IL 60606.

Rogers, Jennifer, et al., edited by Rogers, *Young Adults in School.* Palo Alto, Calif.: Pendragon House, Inc., 1972.

**Career Development**

Bolles, Richard N., *What Color Is Your Parachute?* Berkeley, Calif.: Ten Speed Press, 1977.

Crystal, John C., and Bolles, Richard N., *Where Do I Go from Here with My Life?* New York: Seabury Press, Inc., 1974.

Hawes, Gene and Mark, *Careers Today: A Guide to Challenging, Secure New Jobs with Good Income and Growth Potential, Requiring Two Years Training or Less.* New York: The New American Library, Inc., 1977.

There are literally dozens of books now available which give information about specific careers and how to prepare for entering different fields of interest.

**Coffee House Ministry**

Lillywhite, Byrant, *London Coffee Houses.* Winchester, Mass.: Allen and Unwin, Inc., 1964.

Miller, Alice G., *God Squad*. Wilton, Conn.: Morehouse-Barlow Co., Inc., 1969.

Perry, John D., Jr., *Coffee House Ministry*. Atlanta, Ga.: John Knox Press, 1966.

## Community Study

*Attitude and Opinion Research*. Washington, D.C.: Council for Advancement and Support of Education, 1977.

Backstrom, Charles H., and Hursh, Gerald D., *Survey Research*. Evanston, Ill.: Northwestern University Press, 1963.

Bell, Colin, and Newby, Howard, *Community Studies*. New York: Praeger Publishers, Inc., 1972.

*Community Profile Packet*.
This tells how to study a congregation's community, including: population, age, race, occupation, education, income groups, housing evaluation. Write: Dr. William Kamrath, Concordia Teacher's College, 7400 Augusta Street, River Forest, IL 60305.

Webb, Kenneth, and Hatry, Harry P., *Obtaining Citizen Feedback*. Washington, D.C.: Urban Institute, 1973.

Weinberg, Eve, *Community Surveys with Local Talent: A Handbook*. Chicago: National Opinion Research Center, 1971.

## Divorce

Benham, Arliss R., *The Long Way Back*. Kalamazoo, Mich.: Masters Press, Inc., Division of Merchants Pub. Co., 1977.

Berson, Barbara, and Bova, Ben, *Survival for the Suddenly Single*. New York: St. Martin's Press, Inc., 1974.

Bontrager, G. Edwin, *Divorce and the Faithful Church*. Scottdale, Pa.: Herald Press, 1978.

Bowlby, John, *Separation: Anxiety and Anger*. New York: Basic Books, Inc., Publishers, 1973.

Crook, Roger H., *An Open Book to the Christian Divorcee*. Nashville: Broadman Press, n.d.

Gardner, Richard A., *The Parents Book About Divorce*. Garden City, N.Y.: Doubleday and Co., Inc., 1977.

Hensley, J. Clark, *Coping with Being Single Again.* Nashville: Broadman Press, 1978.

Hudson, R. Lofton, *Til Divorce Do Us Part.* Nashville: Thomas Nelson, Inc., 1974.

Johnson, Stephen M., *First Person Singular: Living the Good Life Alone.* Philadelphia: J. B. Lippincott Company, 1977.

Krantzier, Mel, *Learning to Love Again.* Scranton, Pa.: Thomas Y. Crowell Company, Publishers. Distributed by: Harper & Row, Publishers, Inc., 1977.

Richards, Arlene, and Willis, Irene, *How to Get It Together When Your Parents Are Coming Apart.* New York: Bantam Books, Inc., 1977.

Salk, Lee, *What Every Child Would Like Parents to Know About Divorce.* New York: Harper & Row, Publishers, Inc., 1978.

**Early Adulthood**

*Attitudes, Values and Lifestyles of Young Adults in Greater Dayton: A Summary of the Dayton Young Adult Survey.* Fairborn, Ohio: Miami Valley Young Adult Ministry, 1976.

Levinson, Daniel J., et al., *The Seasons of a Man's Life.* New York: Alfred A. Knopf, Inc., Subs. of Random House, Inc., 1978.

Sheehy, Gail, *Passages.* New York: E. P. Dutton and Elsevier Book Operations, 1976.

Varlejs, Jana, ed., *Young Adult Literature in the Seventies: A Selection of Readings.* Metuchen, N. J.: Scarecrow Press, Inc., Subs. of Grolier Educational Corp., 1978.

**Human Sexuality**

Carney, Clarke G., and McMahon, S. Lynne, eds., *Exploring Contemporary Male-Female Roles: A Facilitator's Guide.* LaJolla, Calif.: University Associates, Inc., 1977.

Hobson, Laura Z., *Consenting Adult.* New York: Doubleday & Co., Inc., 1975.

Mace, David R., *The Christian Response to the Sexual Revolution.* Nashville: Abingdon Press, 1970.

## Life-style: Unmarried Couples

Ashley, Paul P., *Oh Promise Me, but Put It in Writing: Living Together Arrangements Without, During, Before, and After Marriage.* New York: McGraw-Hill Book Company, 1978.

Libby, Roger W., and Whitehurst, Robert N., *Marriage and Alternatives: Exploring Intimate Relationships.* Glenview, Ill.: Scott, Foresman and Co., 1977.

Simons, Joseph, *Living Together: Communication in the Unmarried Relationship.* Chicago: Nelson-Hall, Inc., 1978.

## Marriage

Brenneman, Helen G., *Marriage: Agony and Ecstasy.* Scottdale, Pa.: Herald Press, 1975.

The Caring Series:

Castle, David, *Toward Caring: People Building in the Family.* Richmond, Ind.: Friends United Press, 1973.

Hinshaw, Edwin and Dorothy, *Toward Caring: Couple Enrichment.* Richmond, Ind.: Friends United Press, 1977.

Hinshaw, Ed, and Adams, Charlie, *Toward Caring: Cases and Letters for Dialogue.* Richmond, Ind.: Friends United Press, 1972.

Clinebell, Charlotte H. and Howard J., Jr., *The Intimate Marriage.* New York: Harper & Row, Publishers, Inc., 1970.

DeBurger, James E., ed., *Marriage Today: Problems, Issues and Alternatives.* Cambridge, Mass.: Schenkman Publishing Co., Inc., 1978.

Greenblat, Cathy S., et al., *The Marriage Game: Personal Growth and Fulfillment.* 2nd ed. New York: Random House, Inc., 1977.

Molton, Warren Lane, *Friends, Partners, and Lovers.* Valley Forge: Judson Press, 1979.

Rogers, Carl R., *Becoming Partners: Marriage and Its Alternatives.* New York: Delacorte Press, 1972.

Sammons, David, *The Marriage Option.* Boston: Beacon Press, 1977.

Willimon, William H., *Saying Yes to Marriage*. Valley Forge: Judson Press, 1979.

## Ministry with Young Adults

Anderson, Lowell, ed., *Ministry with Young Adults*. This is a twenty-four page booklet which describes characteristics and trends of young adults and gives helpful guidance for congregational ministry; there is also a bimonthly newsletter with the same title, mailed to congregations and young adult ministry leaders at their request. Write: Division for Parish Services, Lutheran Church in America, 2900 Queen Lane, Philadelphia, PA 19129.

Craig, Floyd, *How to Communicate with Single Adults*. Nashville: Broadman Press, 1978.

Dow, Robert A., *Ministry with Single Adults*. Valley Forge: Judson Press, 1977.

Gillespie, Paul G., "Ministry with Single Young Adults." A reprint from *Baptist Leader,* vol. 40, no. 3 (June, 1978). Available from Judson Book Stores, Valley Forge, PA 19481. Literature Service No. LS14-115.

Hinshaw, Edwin, *Adventuring with Youth*. Write: Friends United Press, 101 Quaker Hill Drive, Richmond, IN 47374.

*Impact.*
A large interreligious network concerned about a number of social issues. Write: Impact, 110 Maryland Avenue, NE, Washington, DC 20002.

Jewett, Dick, *I'm Going to Hitchhike If It's the Last Thing I Do!* Nashville: Southern Publishing Association, 1977.

Johnson, Douglas W., *Single Adult Ministries: A Report on Selected Ministries in the Presbyterian Church in the United States*. Ridgewood, N.J.: Institute for Church Development, Inc., 1978. Write: Institute for Church Development, Inc., 420 Cambridge Road, Ridgewood, NJ 07450.

Knight, Byron, ed., *Developing Ministry with Young Adults*. Pittsburgh: Thesis Cassettes, 1977. Write: Thesis, P.O. Box 11724, Pittsburgh, PA 15228.

Lindsey, Holy Hubert, *Bless Your Dirty Heart: The Famous Street Preacher of the Cal-Berkeley Campus Tells His Story.* Edited by Howard G. Earl. Plainfield, N.J.: Logos International, 1973.

*Ministry with Young Adults.* A packet available from Discipleship Resources, The United Methodist Church, P.O. Box 840, Nashville, TN 37202.
"Ministry with Young Adults in the Local Church," by Lander Beal, a leadership manual included in the packet, is also available separately.

Murphy, Elly, ed., *National Young Adult Reporter.* Published quarterly by the Department of Education, U.S. Catholic Conference, 1312 Massachusetts Avenue, NW, Washington, DC 20005.

Potts, Nancy D., *Counseling with Single Adults.* Nashville: Broadman Press, 1978.

Reed, Bobbie, *Single on Sunday: A Manual for Successful Single Adult Ministries.* St. Louis, Mo.: Concordia Publishing House, 1979.

Wood, Britton, *Single Adults Want to Be the Church, Too.* Nashville: Broadman Press, 1977.

*Young Adult Connection.* A newsletter published in February and August. For information: Young Adult Connection, c/o Clifford E. Kolb, The United Methodist Church, P.O. Box 840, Nashville, TN 37202.

*Young Adult Ministries: A Resource Packet.* Prepared by Young Adult Ministries Committee, Department of Christian Education, Episcopal Diocese of Ohio. Available from Youth and Young Adult Ministries Office, 815 Second Avenue, New York, NY 10017.

*Sound the Call,* a quarterly publication of the Episcopal Young Adult Ministries Network, is also available at this address.

*Young Adult Ministry Resources.* Available from the Department of Education, U. S. Catholic Conference, 1312 Massachusetts Avenue, NW, Washington, DC 20005.

## New Religious Expressions

Biersdorf, John E., *Hunger for Experience: Vital Religious Communities in America Today*. New York: The Seabury Press, Inc., 1975.

Cohen, Daniel, *The New Believers: Young Religion in America*. New York: M. Evans & Co., Inc., 1975.

Cox, Harvey, *Turning East: The Promise and Peril of the New Orientalism*. New York: Simon & Schuster, Inc., 1977.

Ellwood, Robert S., Jr., *Religious and Spiritual Groups in Modern America*. Englewood Cliffs, N.J.: Prentice-Hall, Inc., 1973.

Glock, Charles Y., and Bellah, Robert N., eds., *The New Religious Consciousness*. Berkeley: University of California Press, 1976.

Gribbon, Robert T., *The Problem of Faith-Development in Young Adults*. Write: The Alban Institute, Inc., Mount St. Alban, Washington, DC 20016.

*How to Respond to the Cults*. St. Louis, Mo.: Concordia Publishing House, 1977.

MacCollam, Joel A., *Carnival of Souls: Religious Cults and Young People*. New York: Seabury Press, Inc., 1979.

Needleman, Jacob, *The New Religions*. New York: Doubleday & Co., Inc., 1970; E. P. Dutton and Elsevier Book Operations, 1977.

Streiker, Lowell D., *The Cults Are Coming*. Nashville: Abingdon Press, 1978.

## Organizational Development and Management

Berne, Eric, *The Structure and Dynamics of Organizations and Groups*. New York: Grove Press, Inc., 1966.

Caplow, Theodore, *How to Run Any Organization: A Manual of Practical Sociology*. Hinsdale, Ill.: Dryden Press, Division of Holt, Rinehart and Winston, Inc., 1977.

French, Wendell L., and Bell, Cecil H., Jr., *Organization Development: Behavioral Science Interventions for Organization Improvement*. 2nd ed. New Jersey: Prentice-Hall, Inc., 1978.

Gardiner, M. James, *Program Evaluation in Church Organization.* Winter Park, Fla.: Anna Publishing, Inc., 1977.

Heaton, Herbert, *Productivity in Service Organizations: Organizing for People.* New York: McGraw-Hill Book Company, 1978.

Hendrix, Olan, *Management for the Christian Worker.* Santa Barbara, Calif.: Quill Publications, 1976. Dist. by Mott Media, P.O. Box 236, Milford, MI 48042.

Lendt, David, ed., *The Publicity Process.* 2nd ed. Ames, Iowa: Iowa State University Press, 1975.

Longenecker, Justin G., *Essentials of Management: A Behavioral Approach.* Columbus, Ohio: Charles E. Merrill Publishing Co., Division of Bell and Howell Co., 1977.

Massey, Floyd, Jr., and McKinney, Samuel Berry, *Church Administration in the Black Perspective.* Valley Forge: Judson Press, 1977.

O'Brien, Richard, *Publicity: How to Get It.* New York: Barnes and Noble, Division of Harper & Row., Publishers, Inc., 1978.

Olsson, David E., *Management by Objectives.* Palo Alto, Calif.: Pacific Books, Publishers, 1968.

Sperry, Len, et al., *You Can Make It Happen: A Guide to Self-Actualization and Organizational Change.* Reading, Mass.: Addison-Wesley Publishing Co., Inc., 1977.

Zaltman, Gerald, and Duncan, Robert, *Strategies for Planned Change.* New York: John Wiley and Sons, Inc., 1977.

**Problems of Young Adults**

Alibrandi, Tom, *Young Alcoholics.* Minneapolis, Minn.: CompCare Publications, 1978.

Bennett, Bob, *The Cross and the Needle.* Mountain View, Calif.: Pacific Press Publishing Association, 1972.

Gordon, Suzanne, *Lonely in America.* New York: Simon & Schuster, Inc., 1976.

Leech, Kenneth, *Pastoral Care and the Drug Scene.* Naperville, Ill.: Alec R. Allenson, Inc., 1970.

Morse, Tom, and Lauster, Bobbie, *When the Music Stops.* Old Tappan, N.J.: Fleming H. Revell Company, 1971.

Rothchild, John, and Wolf, Susan, *The Children of the Counterculture.* New York: Doubleday & Co., Inc., 1976.

## Single Life

Christoff, Nicholas B., *Saturday Night, Sunday Morning.* New York: Harper & Row, Publishers, Inc., 1978.

Collins, Gary R., ed., *It's OK to Be Single.* Waco, Texas: Word, Inc., 1976.

Gilder, George, *Naked Nomads: Unmarried Men in America.* New York: Times Books, Div. of The New York Times Book Co., 1974.

Lum, Ada, *Single and Human.* Downers Grove, Ill.: Inter-Varsity Press, 1976.

McGinnis, Marilyn, *Single.* Old Tappan, N.J.: Fleming H. Revell Company, 1974.

Tompkins, Iverna, *How to Be Happy in No Man's Land.* Plainfield, N.J.: Logos International, 1975.

Vetter, Robert, and Vetter, June, *Jesus Was a Single Young Adult.* Elgin, Ill.: David C. Cook Publishing Company, 1978.

## Single Parenting

Adams, Jane, *Sex & the Single Parent.* New York: G. P. Putnam's Sons, 1978.

Bel Geddes, Joan, *How to Parent Alone: A Guide for Single Parents.* New York: Seabury Press, Inc., 1974.

Carter, Velma T., and Leavenworth, J. Lynn, *Putting the Pieces Together.* Valley Forge: Judson Press, 1977. See also *Putting the Pieces Together, Leader's Guide,* for suggestions about group use.

Ferri, Elsa, *Growing up in a One Parent Family.* Atlantic Highlands, N.J.: Humanities Press, Inc., 1976.

Hallett, Kathryn, *A Guide for Single Parents: Transactional Analysis for People in Crisis.* Millbrae, Calif.: Celestial Arts, 1974.

Hope, Karol, and Young, Nancy, *Momma Handbook: The Source for Single Mothers*. New York: The New American Library, Inc., 1976.

Kriesberg, Louis, *Mothers in Poverty: A Study of Fatherless Families*. Chicago: Aldine Publishing Company, 1970.

McFadden, Michael, *Bachelor Fatherhood: How to Raise and Enjoy Your Children As a Single Parent*. New York: Walker & Company, 1974.

Macintyre, Sally, *Single and Pregnant: The Pregnancy Careers of Unmarried Women*. New York: Neale Watson Academic Publications, Inc., 1977.

Pannor, Reuben, et al., *Unmarried Father: New Approaches for Helping Unmarried Young Parents*. New York: Springer Publishing Co., Inc., 1971.

Sauber, Mignon, and Corrigan, Eileen M., *The Six-Year Experience of Unwed Mothers As Parents: A Continuing Study of These Mothers and Their Children*. New York: Community Council of Greater New York, 1970.

Williams, Florence L., *Living As a Single Parent*. Valley Forge: Judson Press, 1976.

Wolley, Persia, *Creative Survival for Single Mothers*. Millbrae, Calif.: Celestial Arts, 1975.

## Widowhood

Jensen, Maxine D., *The Warming of Winter: How the Widow Can Find New Life Beyond Sorrow*. Nashville: Abingdon Press, 1977.

Keelan, Jim, *Re-Entering the Single Life*. Arvada, Colo.: Communications Unlimited, 1977.

Lewis, Alfred A., and Berns, Barrie, *Three Out of Four Wives*. New York: Macmillan, Inc., 1975.

Wiebe, Katie F., *Alone: A Widow's Search for Joy*. Wheaton, Ill.: Tyndale House Publishers, 1976.

Young, Amy R., *By Death or Divorce . . . It Hurts to Lose*. Denver, Colo.: Accent Books, 1976.

## Films

The nearest source for films is quite often the film department of a large public library. For example, the Rundel Library in Rochester, New York, has a huge collection including old-time comedies, feature presentations, and discussion-oriented films. If a library does not have a film collection, perhaps it can provide information as to where various types of films would be available. The following book is a sample of what libraries might have in the way of reference material:

*educational film locator of the consortium of university film centers and r. r. bowker company.* New York and London: R. R. Bowker Company, 1978.
This resource lists and describes approximately 37,000 film titles, tells what university film centers have specific titles, and gives information as to booking addresses, use fees, and availability of catalogs.

Another source for films would be the film departments of denominations. The *American Baptist Films Catalog, 1978-1979,* for instance, lists many subject areas which may be of interest in young adult ministry: alienation, the black experience, Christian education, the church, commitment, communication, community, drugs, ecology, evangelism, the family, freedom, God, human rights, hunger, intergenerational resources, involvement, justice, loneliness, love, mental health, moral values, peace, personhood, poverty, prayer, reconciliation, rural concerns, stewardship, technology, urban concerns, vocations, women, and worship. The resources in this catalog include motion pictures, filmstrips, and recordings. In order to obtain a catalog, write: American Baptist Films, Valley Forge, PA 19481, or Box 23204, Oakland, CA 94623.

A second example is *A Catalog of Religious Films,* a listing of over 500 religious films available for rental. Write: Fortress Church Supply Stores, Lutheran Church in America, 2900 Queen Lane, Philadelphia, PA 19129.

Other denominational addresses can be found by asking pastors who are serving specific denominations, or by consulting the following reference book:

Jacquet, Constant H., ed., *Yearbook of American and Canadian Churches, 1978.* Nashville: Abingdon Press, 1978.

Additional film collections which are highly recommended because they have particularly good discussion-oriented, educational, and/or entertainment-type films are at the following addresses:

Benchmark Films
145 Scarborough Road
Briarcliff Manor, NY 10510

Churchill Films
662 North Robertson Boulevard
Los Angeles, CA 90069

Communication Commission
National Council of Churches of Christ in the U.S.A.
475 Riverside Drive, Room 860
New York, NY 10027

Learning Corporation of America
1350 Avenue of the Americas
New York, NY 10019

Lutheran Film Associates
315 Park Avenue South
New York, NY 10010

McGraw-Hill Films
1221 Avenue of the Americas
New York, NY 10020

Macmillan Films/Audio Brandon Films
34 MacQuesten Parkway South
Mount Vernon, NY 10550

Mass Media Ministries
2116 North Charles Street
Baltimore, MD 21218

Peace Education Program Resources
c/o American Friends Service Committee
1501 Cherry Street
Philadelphia, PA 19102

Perspective Films
369 West Erie Street
Chicago, IL 60610

Phoenix Films
470 Park Avenue South
New York, NY 10016

Pyramid Film Producers
Post Office Box 1048
Santa Monica, CA 90406

United Methodist Communications
1525 McGavock Street
Nashville, TN 37203

Xerox Films
245 Long Hill Road
Middletown, CT 06457

## Funding

This section contains resources which can help the participants of a young adult ministry learn how to raise income by way of special programs, foundation grants, arts agencies and other government agencies, church memberships and organizations, private groups, and individuals.

Before offering a list of these resources, I would like to mention particularly the valuable work of the Foundation Center. In the first place, it has organized a nationwide network of foundation reference collections for free public use. Two libraries contain the Internal Revenue Service returns for all currently active private foundations in the United States: 888 Seventh Avenue, New York, NY 10019 and 1001 Connecticut Avenue, Northwest, Washington, DC 20036. Two other libraries contain the returns of foundations which are located in rather large geographic regions: Western United States (312 Sutter Street, San Francisco, CA 94108), and Midwestern United States (Kent H. Smith Library, 739 National City Bank Building, Cleveland, OH 44114). Then, too, there are more than seventy local, cooperating collections throughout the United States which contain the returns of foundations in those proximities. For information as to locations, write: The Foundation Center, 888 Seventh Avenue, New York, NY 10019.

Secondly, the Foundation Center also publishes a number of very helpful reference books, some of which are the following:

Andrews, F. Emerson, *Philanthropy in the United States: History and Structure.*

*The Foundation Center National Data Book.* Published annually in September, two volumes.

Jacquette, F. Lee and Barbara, *What Makes a Good Proposal?*

Kurzig, Carol, et al., eds., *Foundation Grants to Individuals.* New York: Foundation Ctr., 1977.

Margolin, Judith, B., *About Foundations: How to Find the Facts You Need to Get a Grant.* rev. ed., 1977.

Mayer, Robert A., *What Will a Foundation Look for When You Submit a Grant Proposal?*

All of the resources in the above list can be ordered from: The Foundation Center, 888 Seventh Avenue, New York, NY 10019. Some of the materials from this source are relatively expensive, but the booklets by Andrews, Jacquette, and Mayer are free of charge for up to five copies apiece. One other book which is a standard reference on the subject of grant-making foundations is the following:

Lewis, Marianna O., ed., *The Foundation Directory.*
6th ed. 1977.
Order from: Columbia University Press, 136 South Broadway, Irvington-on-Hudson, NY 10533. This reference will be found in many public libraries.

Other resources which can help in securing funding for young adult ministry are now presented, in alphabetical order.

*Annual Register of Grant Support, 1978-1979.* 12th ed. Chicago: Marquis Academic Media, Marquis Who's Who, Inc., 1978.

Brose, E. F., *Twenty New Ways to Get the Minister Out of Moneyraising.* Austin, Texas: The Sharing Co., 1976.

*Catalog of Federal Domestic Assistance.* Washington, D.C.: United States Printing Office.
For information, write: Superintendent of Documents, United States Government Printing Office, Washington, DC 20402.

Dexter, Kerry, *Bazaars, Fairs and Festivals: A How-to Book.* Wilton, Conn.: Morehouse-Barlow Co., Inc., 1978.

Flanagan, Joan, *The Grass Roots Fundraising Book*. Chicago: The Swallow Press, Inc., 1977.

Golden, Hal, *The Grant Seekers: The Foundation Fund Raising Manual*. Dobbs Ferry, N.Y.: Oceana Publications, Inc., 1976.

Hillman, Howard, and Abarbanel, Karin, *The Art of Winning Foundation Grants*. New York: Vanguard Press, Inc., 1975.

Knudsen, Raymond B., *New Models for Financing the Local Church*. New York: Association Press, 1974.

Lefferts, Robert, *Getting a Grant: How to Write Grant Proposals That Get Results*. Englewood Cliffs, N.J.: Prentice-Hall, Inc., 1978.

Lesjack, John J., *How to Stage a Successful Gold Rush Carnival*. Sacramento, Calif.: Creative Book Company, 1978.

*National Endowment for the Arts: Guide to Programs*. Washington, D.C.: Program Information Office of the National Endowment for the Arts, printed annually. Also contains addresses of state agencies. Write: National Endowment for the Arts, Washington, DC 20506.

Regional Young Adult Project and Pacific Change. *The Bread Game: The Realities of Foundation Fundraising*. rev. ed. San Francisco, Calif.: New Glide Publications, 1974.

*Taft Foundation Reporter*. Regional editions. Washington, D.C.: Taft Corporation, 1978.

Utech, Ingrid, *Stalking the Large Green Giant*. Washington, D.C.: National Youth Alternatives Project, 1976.

## Special Resources

There are also two other kinds of resources which should be mentioned. One is the possibility of attending periodic conferences which are centered upon the theme of young adult ministry. Having attended a national conference entitled "Together in Young Adult Ministry" in 1977 at Barry College, Miami, Florida, I am well aware of the value of intentional gatherings of people who share the same interests of ministry. Other conferences have been developed around the specific themes of youth ministry and ministry with single adults.

All of these afford participants the opportunities of learning together and sharing in the developing field of young adult ministry.

Another very significant source, mentioned in earlier chapters, is the matter of human resources. It just cannot be stressed enough that one of the greatest resources of any young adult ministry is found in the talents, abilities, and commitments of young adult participants. This point needs to be kept in mind whenever people are considering potential resources for ministry.

# Notes

**Chapter 1**

[1] Wade Clark Roof, "Alienation and Apostasy," *Society*, vol. 15, no. 4 (May, June, 1978), p. 44. Published by permission of Transaction, Inc. Copyright © 1978 by Transaction, Inc.

[2] *Ibid.*, p. 43.

[3] Constant H. Jacquet, Jr., ed., *Yearbook of American and Canadian Churches, 1978* (Nashville: Abingdon Press, 1978), pp. 256-257. Used by permission. The statistics are from a 1976 Gallup Poll, but the information was found in this Abingdon Press source.

[4] *Ibid.*, p. 256.

[5] Wade Clark Roof and Christopher Kirk Hadaway, "Review of the Polls: Shifts in Religious Preference—the Mid-Seventies," *Journal for the Scientific Study of Religion*, vol. 16, no. 4 (1977), pp. 409-442. Used by permission. The article indicates that analyses and interpretation of data are drawn from the National Opinion Research Center, the Roper Public Opinion Research Center, and the Survey Archive for the Social Sciences affiliated with the Social and Demographic Research Institute at the University of Massachusetts.

[6] The label "sectarians" is one of the terms which appears in the above article in *JSSR* under the more general heading "Conservative Protestants."

[7] Roof and Hadaway, "Review of the Polls," p. 411.

[8] *Census of Population and Housing* (Washington, D.C.: U.S. Dept. of Commerce, 1970). Census books covering different statistical areas are available, at a cost, from the Superintendent of Documents, U.S. Government Printing Office, Washington, DC 20402.

**Chapter 2**

[1] Gail Sheehy, *Passages: Predictable Crises of Adult Life* (New York: E. P. Dutton & Co., Inc., 1977). Reprinted by permission of E. P. Dutton. Copyright © 1974, 1976 by Gail Sheehy.

[2] *Ibid.*, p. 25.

[3] *Ibid.*, p. 27.

[4] *Ibid.*

[5] *Ibid.*, p. 28.

[6] *Ibid.*
[7] *Ibid.*, p. 27.
[8] *Ibid.*, p. 28.
[9] *Ibid.*, pp. 28-29.
[10] *Ibid.*, p. 30.
[11] *Ibid.*
[12] *The General Mills American Family Report, 1976-77: Raising Children in a Changing Society*, conducted by Yankelovich, Skelly, and White, Inc. (Published by General Mills Consumer Center, n.d.). Appreciation for the use of this material is extended to General Mills, Inc., 9200 Wayzata Boulevard, Minneapolis, MN 55440.
[13] *Ibid.*, p. 28.
[14] *Ibid.*
[15] *Ibid.*, p. 27.
[16] *Ibid.*, p. 28.
[17] *Ibid.*

**Chapter 3**

[1] General Henry M. Robert, *Robert's Rules of Order* (Old Tappan, N.J.: Fleming H. Revell Company, 1967). This work has been published in many editions and is widely available.

**Chapter 5**

[1] Marianna O. Lewis, ed., *The Foundation Directory,* 6th ed. (New York: The Foundation Center, distributed by Columbia University Press, 1977).

# Index